1976

THE NATURE OF CATHOLICITY

THE
NATURE OF CATHOLICITY

by

DANIEL T. JENKINS

(Dr Jenkins
Diasin 2002)

FABER AND FABER LIMITED
24 Russell Square
London

1942

First published in Mcmxlii
by Faber and Faber Limited
24 Russell Square London W.C.1
Second impression November Mcmlxiii
Third impression April Mcmlxvi
Printed in Great Britain
at the Bowering Press Plymouth
All Rights Reserved

PREFATORY NOTE

It is, perhaps, necessary to mention that the purpose of this essay is in no sense to attempt an exposition of the doctrine of the Church proper but merely to state the point of view from which Reformed theology approaches that doctrine. This may help to explain otherwise unaccountable omissions from the treatment and to justify its predominantly critical character.

My deep gratitude is due to several friends who helped in various ways but, in particular, to the Principal of Mansfield College, Oxford, and to the Reverend A. G. Hebert of the Society of the Sacred Mission, Kelham, both of whom very kindly read the book in manuscript form and, while not necessarily agreeing with all its conclusions, gave much encouragement and made many valuable suggestions.

D.T.J.

November 1941

CONTENTS

Chapter I

THE QUESTION IN RECENT DISCUSSION

There is no doubt that in modern England we are witnessing a genuine revival of churchmanship. This is due in part to the theological revival which has spread from the Continent to this country during the last twenty years, but it was well established here long before the dying fires of the Reformation were stirred into life again in Germany and Switzerland. Indeed, even at this time of day, English Christianity continues to combine an extraordinary theological backwardness with a much more developed and self-conscious churchmanship than is frequently found among Reformed theologians on the Continent. It is well known that ever since the beginning of the Oxford Movement, if not before, the English temperament has always found itself more at home in dealing with questions of Church order and administration than with directly theological matters, and generally has found its easiest approach to Dogmatics through concrete issues raised in the course of ordinary

Church life.[1] This tendency has received a further impetus from the rise of the Oecumenical Movement and of a new concern for the relation of the Gospel to the Common Life. The result is that to-day discussion of the doctrine of the Church, in the serious sense of examining differences which are regarded as vitally important because schism is regarded as sinful, is again becoming a major preoccupation of English theologians. That is not to say, as we have already made clear, that the generations of Lightfoot and Hort and Dale or of Gore and Forsyth were not concerned with the doctrine of the Church. But those great figures were, to some extent, exceptions, and it was controversies about Biblical Criticism and 'modern thought' or about secondary issues like ritualism and sectarian education which occupied the centre of the stage. There has been little proper theological controversy about the nature of the Church and of God's ordinance for it since 1662.

It is undeniable that much of our present interest in the doctrine of the Church is due to the witness of the Church of England. Much of this work will be devoted to criticism of positions held in the Church of England, and it is the more important, therefore, that this should be frankly recognized at the outset. The Reformed Churches[2] of the Anglo-Saxon world owe a debt of gratitude to the

[1] Cf. *Doctrine in the Church of England*, p. 25.
[2] This term will be used throughout to refer not only, as is customary, to the Presbyterian Churches alone, but to

Church of England for her constant witness in recent generations to the reality of the Body of Christ when many of them regarded the Church as little more than a convenient form of religious association, and for her preservation and restoration of much of the rich content of the life and worship of the Great Church throughout the ages when again many of them were busy light-heartedly casting away their heritage through ignorance of its true value. If we are able to claim that in 1662 it was the Ejected Ministers who were the true witnesses on behalf of the reality of the Body of Christ, we have to admit that in the nineteenth and early twentieth centuries it has frequently been the Catholic Anglicans who have stood in their succession. No doubt the Oxford Movement owes more than it is sometimes ready to allow to Methodism and the Evangelical Revival, and no doubt its extravagances have often served to wound the Body rather than to build it up, but nevertheless it is largely through its work that churchmanship has revived in England. It is because of what it has achieved that we who belong to a different tradition and who have recovered our concern for churchmanship from another source find it easier than do many of our brethren on the Continent and in America to ponder upon the meaning of the great words 'Catholic' and 'Apostolic'. As Dr. Visser t'Hooft put it, writing on the threshold of

all Churches which officially accept the principle of Reformation according to the Word of God.

9

the present Protestant theological revival, 'Protestantism as it is to-day does not take the visible Church seriously. To be sure, it is as much preoccupied with ecclesiastical affairs as any other Christian confession. But to take the Church seriously is more than to be concerned over questions of order and organization. It is to conceive of the concrete, given Church as the normal channel of God's grace. It is to believe in it as a particular gift of God, an indispensable element of His plan of salvation.'[1] There is really only one question with various aspects (which non-Roman Catholicism puts to Protestantism), 'Does Protestantism take the visible Church seriously?'[2]

But although the question of the nature of the Church has thus been brought inescapably before our notice, and although many books have been written about Catholicism and what it means, there have been extraordinarily few attempts to state precisely what gives the quality of catholicity to the Church. Even the Report of the Edinburgh Faith and Order Conference carefully avoids making an explicit assertion regarding the nature of catholicity. And, for the most part, while Anglo-Catholics are definite enough in saying what they consider the marks of catholicity to be, they are noticeably reluctant to state what the quality of catholicity is or to make clear the inwardness of its relation to the Gospel. Sometimes, indeed, they

[1] Dr. Visser t'Hooft, *Anglo-Catholicism and Orthodoxy* (S.C.M., 1929), p. 159.　　[2] Ibid., p. 158.

go so far as to justify, with what seems to us to be almost a *reductio ad absurdum* of the English 'distrust of definition', their vagueness on this point on the ground that catholicity is a fact which, like life, we cannot explain but have to accept.[1] Generally, however, they have contented themselves with defending their Church's catholicity on traditionalist grounds and leaving it at that. With characteristic English 'moderation' and 'good sense' they have appealed to Scripture and Christian antiquity. There they claimed to find a justification for their conception of Catholic liturgy and order, and any criticism they met with historical arguments. Since it was the doctrine of the Ministry which was the chief point of difference between them and English Protestantism, which in its orthodox form was able to agree with most of the Thirty-Nine Articles, they emphasized pre-eminently the importance of episcopacy as a mark of catholicity, but once again it was a simple historical appeal to the fact that the episcopal ministry had always been a mark of the Great Church, and was regarded as a symbol of catholicity in Patristic times which served as their justification. And their quarrel with the position of the Roman Church, with its perfectly clear definition of catholicity as being in communion with the see of Rome, was, similarly, that there was no historical basis for the Roman claims in Christian antiquity.

[1] As by Dr. T. A. Lacey in *The Anglo-Catholic Faith* (Methuen), pp. 76–7.

Conversations about re-union, the uncertainties of the findings of Patristic scholarship and increasing theological self-consciousness have compelled development from this somewhat naïve position. On one side there has been a tendency to find the basis of catholicity in the so-called 'branch' theory of the Church, in the way the main Churches of Christendom throughout the centuries developed. The three great Catholicisms, Latin Christendom, Eastern Christendom, Northern Christendom, are each held to be a characteristic expression of the one Faith in terms of differing temperaments and traditions and to prove their catholicity by their permanence and dominating influence, as well as by their possession of Scripture, Creeds, Sacraments, and episcopacy.[1] This necessarily vague but widely influential tendency, with its affinities with historical Romanticism and the so-called 'Incarnational' theology, is a development of the Anglican doctrine of catholicity in the direction of Liberalism. But on the other side, there has been a development in the opposite direction. Instead of looking outwards from Scripture, Creeds, Sacraments and episcopacy to the visible historic form of the Church, an increasing number of Anglican theologians have been looking inwards to discover the relation between Scripture, Creeds, Sacraments and episcopacy and the Gospel which they express, and have sought to show how traditional Catholic Church order is justifiable because it is an expres-

[1] Cf. *Northern Catholicism*, ed. N. P. Williams (S.P.C.K.).

sion of Jesus Christ, God's revelation of Himself to men. The most notable and detailed example of this approach is Professor Michael Ramsey's *The Gospel and the Catholic Church*, which insists, in the opening words of the preface, 'that the meaning of the Christian Church becomes most clear when it is studied in terms of the Death and Resurrection of Jesus Christ'. The significance of the rise and growing power of this point of view[1] we are only just beginning to grasp, but one thing is clear about it. Its criterion of the nature of catholicity is theological and not merely historical. This makes discussion with modern Reformed churchmen possible at once, and removes the dreary deadlocks familiar in conversations about Reunion because the parties concerned are at cross-purposes. For the fundamental position of Reformed churchmen also is that the nature of catholicity can be determined only in the light of God's Word, Jesus Christ, and that Church Order has significance only in relation to the Gospel. This was the issue at the Reformation, though all its implications were perhaps not grasped even then, and when modern theologians in the Catholic branch of the Church of England accept it also then the stage is set for the most promising and fruitful discussion of the last three hundred years. And the fact that in recent generations Reformed churchmen have been

---

[1] It is represented also, though less directly than in Professor Ramsey's book, in the works of Father A. G. Hebert and in Mr. Donald MacKinnon's *The Church of God*.

little interested in questions of catholicity and indeed, in many cases, have not believed in the Church in any recognizable Biblical or traditional sense, makes us all the more grateful for this revival of theological interpretation of Church Order in the Church of England. They have the advantage over many of us of standing in a tradition which for many generations now has been intensely preoccupied with questions of Church Order and in their own Church life have already experienced some of the fullness of liturgical life which our Fathers also knew but which we, their sons, have frittered away. In our revival of Reformed churchmanship which has come primarily from a study of the Bible and of Dogmatic Theology, we have therefore much to learn from them.

At the same time, however, there is a certain difference of approach and emphasis between modern Reformed theologians and even these theologically minded members of the Church of England. It is not merely that we, who in England belong mainly, though not entirely, to the so-called 'Free Churches', speak out of a different tradition from theirs. It is that our whole approach is more directly theological in the narrower sense. We start from the question of the nature of Dogmatics and the doctrine of God and of redemption and work out towards the doctrine of the Church. That is why, after several years of the Reformed revival, we are only now beginning to treat the doctrine of the Church with something like the same seriousness as the doctrine of revelation.[1] They, on the other hand, tend to start from the fact of the Church and its traditional order and work back from that to considering its relation to the Gospel, often without undergoing the tremendous critical discipline which Reformed Dogmatics imposes on those who endeavour to ascertain the nature of the Gospel, but contenting themselves with appeal to the words of Scripture and Biblical Theology in its simple form. This, for example, is very much the method of Ramsey. The result is that while there is a strong affinity between us, we tend never quite to get to grips with each other. Reformed theologians are always grateful to Catholic Anglicans for the way in which they have so fully articulated the doctrine of the Church and, frequently, for the solid way in which they attach themselves to the Scriptures, but they are puzzled by their apparent obliviousness to theological issues which seem to them of burning importance.[2] These, such as the distinction between the Church and the Word and the principle of Reformation according to the Word of God and the significance of natural theology and the question of à *theologia gloriae* and a *theologia viatoris*, have decisive significance to

[1] It is significant that Barth called the first edition of his Dogmatic (1927), *Christliche Dogmatik*, but changed the title of the second edition (1932) to *Kirchliche Dogmatik*.

[2] E.g. Ramsey's discussion of the Reformation and of Barth.

Reformed theologians for their whole conception of the Church, Ministry, Sacraments, the authority of Scripture, and all else. We are not sure, therefore, whether we ultimately agree with each other or not. It is certain that the discussion has taken a more hopeful turn than it has for centuries. It is certain that we all have much to learn from each other. Most of us would agree that our own traditions are not in themselves adequate[1] and that we are working together to a new and deeper understanding of the nature of the Gospel and of the Church. But in order to do that it is essential that we should enunciate as clearly as possible our own positions and our difficulties about the positions of others. Inevitably, and indeed properly, controversial as what follows will be, it is intended primarily to promote the discussion between Reformed and Catholic Anglican theologians, which the author regards as the most important and fruitful now engaging our minds in England. He is encouraged to believe that Catholic Anglicans will, at least, not find his language strange because of so many encouraging signs of a revival of interest in Dogmatic Theology among younger Anglicans.[2] It seems hardly credible that we who have so much in common and speak in such similar terms, both in our criticisms of recent theology and churchman-

[1] Cf. Ramsey, *The Gospel and the Catholic Church*, ch. xiii.
[2] Cf. the discussion on Younger and Older Anglican theologians initiated by the Archbishop of York in *Theology*, November 1939.

ship and in our own attempts to express theological truth and define Church Order, can be in ultimate disagreement. There will be many in the Church of England and many more in the 'Free' Churches who, if they trouble to read this book, will be angered and disgusted by it. But, through the mercy of God, there will be some in both camps who will at least understand what it is brokenly trying to say. If it in any way helps to remove the miserable and enervating divisions which now force us into unreal separation, and make more manifest the marks of that one holy Catholic and Apostolic Church so grievously disfigured in our midst while the world is perishing for the lack of it, the author will be well rewarded.

Chapter II

THE APOSTOLIC SUCCESSION

I

Firstly, we must define the quality of catholicity. The title 'Catholic' was first applied to the Church, as *Doctrine in the Church of England*[1] reminds us, in the Epistles of Ignatius, where it meant, in the words of Lightfoot, 'the general or universal Church, as opposed to a particular body of Christians'. Gradually, however, it came to have the meaning of the Church which was the faithful custodian of the Apostolic tradition as against the heretical sects who from time to time broke away from it. The Church which claims the title 'Catholic' claims, above all else, to be the true Church, in whose fold all true believers are found. The quality of catholicity, then, is that quality in the Church which is the essence of its nature as the Church, the quality without which it is not recognizable as the Church and which, therefore, is the common possession of all Churches which are Churches. Catholicity is linked up with the idea of universality because it is the quality which

[1] Page 109.

18

all Churches, however much they may differ from each other in other ways, must possess if they are to lay claim to the name of 'Church'.[1] Thus the inquiry into the nature of catholicity is the same as that into the nature of the true Church.

That is the primary meaning of catholicity, and the one which will occupy our attention in this chapter. But there is a secondary meaning, which develops naturally out of the first, and with which we shall have to deal later. It is concerned not merely with the *essence* of the Church, but also with its *fullness*. Just because it is the true and universal Church, the Catholic Church bears all the marks of the Church. It is completely the Church, lacking none of the attributes of the Church, and no body can be more fully the Church than it.[2] This we shall endeavour to develop in our fourth chapter.

The Gospel of God is Jesus Christ. Where Christ is, His Church is. *Ubi Christus ibi ecclesia*. That is

[1] 'For that is truly and in the strictest sense "Catholic" which, as the name itself and the reason of the thing declare, comprehends all universally.' (Vincent of Lerins, *Commonitorium*, ii, 6.)

[2] Dr. A. E. J. Rawlinson is surprisingly halting and vague in putting this point when he says: 'Catholicism stands, according to its true idea, both for the presentation of the Gospel of Jesus Christ in its fulness, and also for a certain wholeness, a certain completeness, in the development, maintenance and building-up of Christianity as a system and spiritual way or manner of life.' *Essays Catholic and Critical* (S.P.C.K.), p. 89.

the beginning and the end of our argument. The baptismal confession, 'Jesus is Lord', marks the foundation of the Church; the words of Institution, 'This is my body which is for you', mark the continuance of the Church; and the 'summing-up of all things in Christ' in 'the fulness of the times' marks the consummation of the Church. It is clear, therefore, that the inquiry into the nature of catholicity and thus into the nature of the true Church is the same as the question, 'Is Jesus Christ in the Church?'

This all bodies which lay claim to the name of Church would readily accept. The familiar tag, *Ubi Christus ibi ecclesia*, is heard as much from the lips of Roman Catholics or of 'Liberal Modernists' as from Reformed churchmen. The purpose of this essay, however, is to attempt to bring out the meaning of that phrase in such a way as to raise the question of whether all branches of the Church take it with sufficient seriousness. This is not a work of 'regular Dogmatics,'[1] although the question of the nature of catholicity is, ultimately, the primary concern of 'regular Dogmatics' also, and we shall do no more than glance at the way in which our question and the related question of Church Order are bound up with our attitude to Natural Theology and with the modern attempt to explain away the confession 'Jesus is Lord' in a

[1] Cf. the distinction between 'regular' and 'irregular' Dogmatics in Barth, *Dogmatic* (English translation, T. & T. Clark), i, 1, p. 318.

fashion which denies the seriousness of the de-
nunciation of idols in the First Commandment,
but our claim will be that defective catholicity is
always due to saying 'Jesus Christ—and' or 'Jesus
Christ—but' and not 'always and only Jesus
Christ'. It is the Jesus Christ who came 'in the
flesh', with all the stubborn historicity and particularity which the Fourth Gospel implies by that
phrase, Who alone makes the Church to be the true
Church of God. 'No man hath seen God at any
time; the only-begotten Son, which is in the bosom
of the Father, he hath declared him.'[1] 'And in
none other is there salvation: for neither is there
any other name under heaven that is given among
men wherein we must be saved.'[2]

But how do we know the Jesus Christ Who came
'in the flesh'? The answer can be given unequivocally—through the testimony of the Apostles
and through the witness of the prophets, whose
function is now fulfilled in that of the Apostles.
The supreme mark of a Church's catholicity is its
acceptance of and continuity with the testimony
of the Apostles. To be Catholic the Church must
also be Apostolic. At this early stage, therefore,
our position is marked off from that of the 'Liberal
Modernists', whose characteristic principle, however much it may be modified in particular cases,
is a denial of the testimony of the Apostles. Using
the methods of the modern philosophy of 'the

[1] John i. 18.
[2] Acts iv. 12.

science of history', their aim is to go behind the testimony of the Apostles to their risen Lord to a 'Jesus of history' whom they claim to rediscover in the Synoptic Gospels, a Jesus who has been obscured for us by the complicated theological interpretation of the Apostles, pre-eminently Saint Paul and Saint John, and the Early Church as a whole.[1] As against this position, the Protestant Churches owe a great debt of gratitude to the Churches of traditional Catholicism for their insistence in recent generations on the fact of the Church's apostolicity. 'That which was from the beginning, that which we have heard, that which we have seen with our eyes, that which we beheld, and our hands handled, concerning the Word of life (and the life was manifested and we have seen, and bear witness and declare unto you the life, the eternal life, which was with the Father and was manifested unto us); that which we have seen and heard declare we unto you also, that ye also may have fellowship with us: yea, and our fellowship is with the Father, and with his Son Jesus Christ.'[2] These solemn opening words of the first Epistle of John, where, as Hoskyns reminds us, the 'we' undoubtedly refers to the apostolic com-

[1] Cf. Mr. Frank Lenwood's *Jesus, Lord and Leader* (Constable, 1930). It is difficult, at this time of day, to understand the mentality which could thus calmly set aside so much of the New Testament as well as nineteen hundred years of the Church's life and thought.

[2] 1 John i. 1-3.

munity,[1] make abundantly clear the central place which the authority of the Apostles holds in the life of the Church. It is true that Saint Paul in the opening chapters of Galatians pours scorn upon those who maintained that a certain kind of connection with the Apostles was necessary before his 'gospel' could be accepted. The passage is of crucial importance for the Reformed doctrine of catholicity as against that of traditional Catholicism, and we are not likely to minimize its significance, but it in no way denies the fact of apostolic authority. It confirms it rather, and throws important light on its true nature. What Saint Paul says is that his 'gospel' is of equal validity with that of the 'Jerusalem authorities' because he also had received an apostolic commission of the same kind as theirs. He had seen the risen Lord on the Damascus road, and therefore he had become one of the company of the Apostles, even though as one born out of due time and as the least of the Apostles.[2] In order to justify to his readers his preaching of the Gospel to the Gentiles he has first to justify his own apostolic authority. Similarly, whenever Paul is conveying to his readers one of the central truths of the Gospel, he is at pains to remind his readers, as Dr. A. M. Hunter has recently pointed out,[3] that what he is telling them is

[1] Sir Edwyn Hoskyns, *The Fourth Gospel* (Faber), p. 46.
[2] 1 Cor. xv. 8–9.
[3] In *Paul and His Predecessors* (Nicholson & Watson, 1940).

23

part of the apostolic tradition, and that to reject it is equivalent to rejecting Christ.[1] Professor Dodd has shown us the unity of the apostolic preaching from the earliest times, a unity which dominates the New Testament, and it is a commonplace of Early Church history, setting aside for the moment the question of the exact sense in which the episcopate was thought of as the organ through which apostolic authority was expressed, that the acid test of the catholicity of any doctrine was, always, 'Is it the teaching of the Apostles?'[2]

We are as ready, therefore, as traditional Catholicism is, to assert that apostolicity is the essential mark of catholicity, but our position is distinguished from theirs by the fact that we are compelled to insist that it is their *testimony* which constitutes the Apostles as Apostles. The testimony does not draw its authority from the fact that it is the Apostles who bear it, as traditional Catholic teaching seems to suggest, but the Apostles have authority only in so far as they forget themselves in being faithful witnesses to Jesus Christ. Like John the Baptist in the Isenheimer altar-piece so beloved of Barth, they are, from one side, significant only as hands pointing away from themselves to the figure of Christ on the cross. It is not their faith or their zeal or their religious genius or any special charismata they possessed, like the gift of the Spirit by the laying on of hands, and certainly not any acci-

[1] 1 Cor. xi. 23–5 and xv. 1–11 are striking examples.
[2] Irenaeus, *Contra Haeresios*.

dent of historical association, but their *testimony*[1] which constitutes them Apostles. This is what the argument of Saint Paul in the first two chapters of Galatians already mentioned makes clear. He is 'an Apostle (not from men neither through a man but through Jesus Christ, and God the Father, who raised him from the dead)'.[2] Because of that he is able to expose the pretensions with which certain people were surrounding the persons of the Apostles at Jerusalem. It is true that if Paul's 'gospel' had, in the first place, been fundamentally different from their 'gospel', then there would have been a *prima facie* case against Paul's 'gospel', but since it was the same Christ Who had appeared to both, then the Jerusalem Apostles had no greater authority than Paul, for it was the presence of the living Christ which gave them both their authority. Traditional Catholics may resent the apparent 'irregularity' of Paul's call to the Apostolate, but there is no doubt that the Jerusalem Apostles accepted his claim.[3] It is hard to believe that the exceptional circumstances of Paul's call are not intended as a reminder to a Church which is always in danger of forgetting it that it is their testimony

[1] 'In the transitory conditions of authority between man and man *qua* man, authority will normally be physically recognizable by power. An Apostle has no other proof than his own statement, and at the most his willingness to suffer anything for the sake of that statement.' S. Kierkegaard, *Of the Difference between a Genius and an Apostle* (English translation in *The Present Age*, Oxford 1940, p. 159).

[2] Gal. i. 1.   [3] Gal. ii. 7–10.

to a God who retains His Lordship over them and therefore His freedom to work independently of them or even against them which gives their authority to His ministers. This, surely, is also the point of the story of the denial of Peter, which all four evangelists are at pains to record. Simon, the son of Jonah, before he can become Peter, the rock on which Christ builds His Church, must be made to see that he and all his conviction of his unique spiritual importance—'though all should deny thee yet will I not deny thee'—must die and be born again through the free grace of the Master he betrayed. Peter had cause to know, if ever man did, that it was his testimony alone which made him an Apostle, and his story was written for our learning.[1] And the same truth is underlined in the symbolism of the wonderful and mysterious story of the Resurrection Appearance to the seven disciples at the sea of Tiberias in John xxi. Of themselves, having fled from the scene of the crucifixion, they can do nothing. All night they cast their nets in vain. But, when they cast their nets in obedience to their Lord's instruction, and so completely have they rejected Him that at first they do not even recognize Him as their Lord, their nets are filled with the hundred and fifty-three fishes. And the sacramental meal is prepared by Him, independently of them, while they are so ashamed in His

[1] Cf. also Cyril of Alexandria's comment on John xxi. 15–19, quoted in Hoskyns, *The Fourth Gospel*, p. 666, and contrasted with Roman Catholic exegesis of this passage.

presence at their own unbelief that they dare not
name the name of the Lord, and it is at His invita-
tion that they take and eat. As Hoskyns put it,
'There is no free and independent apostolic position. In the Johannine Writings the Apostles are
neither great men, nor are they heroes. No single
one of them—not even Peter, not even the Beloved
Disciple—provides the author with a suitable
theme for the exercise of any latent biographical
skill he may have possessed. The original disciples
form the link between Jesus and the believing
Christians; they have no other importance, no
other right to exist. They *followed* and *saw*. They
followed *Jesus* (i. 37–42, xxi. 19–22); and they
saw *his glory* (i. 14, 15). For this reason, in the
gospel, the pronoun "ego" belongs rightly only
to Jesus. He alone speaks with proper authority,
and only in dependence upon Him do the pro-
nouns "we" and, in the Epistle, "I" possess any
abiding significance.'[1] Once again, as the protagonists of a sacrificing priesthood as against a
preaching ministry cannot very well deny, it is
surely significant that the apostolic commission,
directly in Saint Mark[2] and Saint Luke[3] and by
implication in Saint Matthew,[4] is to *preach* the
Gospel and that as a matter of fact we do find the
Apostles, in the early chapters of the Book of Acts,
engaged in preaching as their primary activity—
'and every day in the temple and at home they did

[1] *The Fourth Gospel*, p. 101.   [2] xvi. 15.
[3] xxiv. 46–9.   [4] xxviii. 19–20.

not cease to teach and to preach Jesus as the Christ'.[1] Traditional Catholicism will not deny all this, but we are bound to inquire, as we must later in a different context, whether, to say the least of it, it takes it with sufficient seriousness.

Since, then, apostolicity is the mark of catholicity, and the Apostle is what he is in virtue of his testimony to the risen Christ, the test of a Church's catholicity is always whether its testimony to Jesus Christ is the same as that of the Apostles, 'the eye-witnesses of His majesty'. This immediately raises the further question, 'What means have we of knowing what the testimony of the Apostles actually was?' And the answer to this question can be given equally unequivocally. The Apostles themselves took care to ensure that we should be left in no doubt as to the nature of their testimony. They left us the Holy Scriptures. They themselves would pass away and would be unable to exercise their authority in person in our midst any more, but they would leave us their solemn testimony to the words and works, the death and resurrection of Jesus Christ their Lord, and with that in our hands we should be able to discern the truly apostolic preaching from the false and thus the Church of Christ from that of anti-Christ. 'Forasmuch as many have taken in hand to draw up a narrative concerning those matters which have been fulfilled among us, even as they delivered them unto us, which from the beginning

[1] Acts v. 42.

28

were eye-witnesses and ministers of the word, it seemed good to me also, having traced the course of all things accurately from the first, to write unto thee in order, most excellent Theophilus; that thou mightest know the certainty concerning the things wherein thou wast instructed.'[1] As Hoskyns says of the Fourth Gospel, 'and so, behind the author of the Fourth Gospel, there lies a witness by word and by pen which it is his purpose to preserve and to present to his readers as possessing supreme authority. . . . It is their [the original disciples'] witness, rather than some esoteric or meditative authority of his own, that enables the author of the Johannine Writings to exercise authority; and it is this same apostolic witness, rather than any authority inhering in a growing organism, that is able to bind the whole believing Christian community into one fellowship, and to provide it with the capacity to make known to the world the meaning of the mission of Jesus and to declare the love of God.'[2] 'Holy Scripture is a *token* of revelation. Unbelief is possible even when confronted by this token. But there has never yet been a faith in the revelation which has passed by this token, a faith which was not rather awakened, nourished, and controlled precisely through the instrumentality of this token.'[3] Yet even in the compilation of the

[1] Luke i. 1.

[2] *The Fourth Gospel*, pp. 96–7.

[3] K. Barth in *Revelation* (ed. Baillie & Martin, Faber), p. 68.

record itself they do not allow themselves to lose sight of the fact that it is in the Lord to Whom they bear testimony and not in themselves as witnesses that the authority resides. In the Fourth Gospel the identity of the author has been completely lost in the witness, but in the less formal Pauline epistles we can see how their minds work. In the well-known passage in 1 Corinthians where the Apostle discusses various problems connected with marriage[1] he commands authoritatively where there is a clear saying of the Lord to guide him, but where there is not he is careful to point out that he is speaking only in his own right. 'But to the rest say I, not the Lord.' And there is, of course, the powerful passage in Galatians (i. 12) on which Luther comments, 'But thou wilt say, the Church is holy, the fathers are holy. It is true, notwithstanding, albeit the Church be holy, yet is it compelled to pray: "Forgive us our trespasses." So, though the fathers be holy, yet are they saved by the forgiveness of sins. Therefore neither am I to be believed, nor the Church, nor the fathers, nor the Apostles, no, nor an angel from heaven, if we teach anything against the Word of God.'[2] Because of this the Reformers insisted that 'we do require a succession of doctrine, not of persons, even of the prophetical and apostolical doctrine, so that of necessity we must run again to the books

[1] 1 Cor. vii. 1–12.
[2] Luther, *The Epistle to the Galatians* (ed. J. P. Fallowes, Harrison Trust), p. 33.

of the Prophets and Apostles for the proof of the true succession.'[1]

Here again, however, it is important that we should have the right attitude to the Scriptures and that we should understand the kind of authority the Apostles, and after them the Church in defining the Canon, claimed for them. It is more or less generally agreed, except in circles which need not concern us in this discussion, that the Scriptures are not self-explanatory nor merely a series of detailed scientific 'proofs' nor a compendium of clear-cut rules, that, in fact, they need *exegesis*. And again, it is accepted in a general way that Jesus Christ provides the key to their interpretation. But the method of arriving at the meaning of the Scriptures commonly adopted both by 'Liberal Protestants' and 'Liberal Catholics'—and frequently by the 'Conservatives' in both camps also in their attempts to confute them—shows that they have not understood what was involved in the knowledge of Jesus Christ which the Apostles mean to convey. They have assumed that the true meaning of the Scriptures could be ascertained by a 'detached' study of what it says and that the truth of the Apostles' testimony could be judged by the methods of scientific proof familiar to us from other disciplines. But this overlooks the fact

[1] Beza, *An Exhortation to the Reformation of the Church* (1565). Quoted in Ainslie, *Doctrine of Ministerial Order in the Reformers of the sixteenth and seventeenth centuries* (T. & T. Clark), pp. 219–20.

that, as the Apostles intended, the Scriptures are a 'token of revelation'. It is true that in so far as the Scriptures are literary and historical documents composed by human beings like ourselves they will respond to the methods of literary and historical criticism, which, just because Jesus Christ truly came 'in the flesh', will help to illuminate their meaning by helping us to understand their context. Nevertheless, since the Scriptures testify of God, the Lord, Whose ways are not as our ways nor His thoughts as our thoughts, to apply the methods of scientific criticism alone to their interpretation is false and unscientific because it does not take cognizance of the unique nature of the subject-matter. Scientific criticism cannot lay hold on the revelation, and to imagine that it can means only that the critic is allowing his own uncritically-held presuppositions—in the case of the Liberal Protestant those of his peculiar mental environment and in the case of the Liberal Catholic the more reliable ones of his Church tradition as he knows it—to guide him in his interpretation, and is not allowing the Scriptures, with their profound fusion of history and theological interpretation which is the unique contribution of the Apostles, to speak their own message to him. As Hoskyns puts it of the attitude of the author of the Fourth Gospel to his readers—we quote at length because the passage is peculiarly apposite:

'The Fourth Gospel is a universal, a catholic book. Though no doubt it was originally addressed to particular men and women, yet its author does not for one moment intend these especial readers to suppose that his work concerns them only. He claims to be setting forth the Truth, the veritable Gospel, not *a* truth or *a* gospel. . . . But when this is said, the modern reader must by an effort of historical imagination first endeavour to place himself in the position of those for whom the Gospel was originally written. Only he must not rest until this position is found to be charged with universal significance, until he stands here naturally because it is his inevitable position as a man. He must not rest until he stands where the Jews once stood and did not apprehend, and where Abraham and Isaiah once stood and did apprehend, until he stands confronted, not by the evolution of history, not even by the development of the Church but by the Last Hour; until that is to say, he stands confronted by the Truth, until the present time is confronted by eternity, and until the present place is met by the meaning of history— in fact until he stands before God.'[1]

That is to say, the Apostles would not have regarded their testimony as true testimony unless it brought those who read face to face with the Subject of the testimony—the living God in Jesus Christ. They would have said that it had been misunderstood as the Jews persistently misunderstood it unless the 'critic' was driven by it to stand under the κρίσις of Jesus Christ, God's

[1] Hoskyns, *The Fourth Gospel*, pp. 44 and 45.

Word, and, and, knowing his own sin of unbelief, to cry 'My Lord and my God' and receive Him in faith. It is only when the discipline of this κρίσις is undergone that we are in a position to understand the Scriptures and produce properly theological exegesis and therefore to stand in the succession of the Apostles, for—as we have already made clear—as a condition of their apostolate, of their being able to testify, they, too, underwent the same discipline, having repented and received remission of sins, having died and become new creations in Jesus Christ.

II

Now our argument gathers to a head. Apostolicity is the mark of catholicity. And the apostolic office consists in testimony to Jesus Christ, His words and works, His death and resurrection, as the life of the Church. The testimony of the Apostles we now possess in the form of the Holy Scriptures, which are their legacy to us. But the Scriptures, as we have seen, are not self-evidencing. They are not the revelation itself, Jesus Christ is the revelation, but they are the indispensable token of the revelation. They are understood as testimony, which is the sense in which the Apostles meant them to be understood, only to those who have heard Jesus Christ speaking through them and have obeyed His voice. How then, is it possible to hear the voice of Jesus Christ speaking through

the Scriptures? The answer of the Scriptures themselves and indeed of the Church throughout its
history, has been only one—through the Holy
Ghost. 'No man can say Jesus is Lord but in the
Holy Spirit.'[1] 'But the Paraclete, even the Holy
Spirit, whom the Father will send in my name, he
shall teach you all things, and bring to your re-
membrance all that I said unto you.'[2] 'The Paraclete,' says Hoskyns, 'who is the Holy Spirit, will
remind the believers of the Lord's teaching (ii. 22;
xii. 16; xiii. 7): and yet His work is more than a
reminiscence of the *ipsissima verba* of the Son of
God: it is a living representation of all that He had
once spoken to His disciples, a creative exposition
of the Gospel.'[3] Therefore, as Forsyth used to say,
the Holy Ghost is the 'Highest Critic'. And we
can put it even more boldly than that. It is the
personal presence of God with us through Jesus
Christ. It is 'the light of the knowledge of God in
the face of Jesus Christ', the subjective side of
revelation. It is, as the culmination of the Gospel
story in Pentecost makes clear, God's Lordship,
proclaimed by the prophets, manifest in Jesus
Christ, witnessed to by the Apostles and established in us. Through the Holy Ghost, then, we
are able to stand where the Apostles stood and
say 'Amen' to their testimony. It is through
the Holy Ghost that we know their words, the
Scriptures, to be in truth God's Word because

[1] I Cor. xii. 3.   [2] John xiv. 26.
[3] *The Fourth Gospel*, p. 543.

through the Holy Ghost we have heard God's Word, Jesus Christ, speaking to us in the Scriptures.[1]

From the foregoing account it will, perhaps, be a little clearer what Reformed theologians mean by the 'Catholicism of the Word'.[2] Jesus Christ is God's Word (John i. 1) and the Scriptures can be spoken of, secondarily and derivatively, as God's Word in so far as they declare Jesus Christ, and preaching is God's Word in so far as it presents the Jesus Christ Who is in the Scriptures as our 'contemporary', and the Sacraments are God's Word in so far as we receive Jesus Christ in our hearts by faith, which is the work of the Holy Ghost. We shall go on to attempt to explain how Jesus Christ, the life of the Church, expresses Himself in the form of the Church in such a way that we are able to recognize the Church's catholicity. At this point our concern is to emphasize, as our first conclusion which is of decisive importance for our whole inquiry, that catholicity does inhere in Jesus Christ, God's Word, and nowhere else. Where He is not present as Lord, the Church is not present and a body which does not possess Christ possesses none of the marks of the true Church. 'But if any man hath not the Spirit of

[1] Cf. Barth in *Revelation* and the great Essay on the Trinity in the *Dogmatic*, i, 1.
[2] Nathaniel Micklem, *What is the Faith?* (Hodder & Stoughton), pp. 215–16.

36

Christ, he is none of his.'[1] Therefore the Scots Confession of 1560 says:[2]

'The notes, signs and assured tokens whereby the immaculate Spouse of Christ Jesus is knawen fra the horrible harlot, the kirk malignant, we affirme, are nouther Antiquitie, Title usurpit, lineal Descence, Place appointed, nor multitude of men approving ane error. For Cain, in age and title, was preferred to Abel and Seth: Jerusalem had prerogatives above all places of the eird, where alswa were the Priests lineally descended fra Aaron, and greater number followed the Scribes, Pharisies and Priests, then unfainedly beleeved and approved Christ Jesus and His doctrine.'

That is why Reformed theology prefers to speak of a Catholicism of the Word rather than of Apostolic Succession. It is because of the danger of concentrating on non-essential or false connections with the Apostles. It is by making Scripture the rule of faith that the Reformed Church stands in the true Apostolic Succession. For, as we have tried to show, in leaving us the Scriptures the Apostles wanted to make clear that their authority did not inhere, as Hoskyns says, 'in the growing organism of the Church', but in Jesus Christ, from Whom the Church takes its life and Who yet always stands over against the Church in judgement and in promise. They wanted themselves to

[1] Rom. viii. 9.
[2] Art. XVIII, quoted in Barth, *The Knowledge of God and the Service of God* (Hodder & Stoughton), p. 161.

be forgotten and their testimony to remain, lest their testimony, and hence their true apostolic function, be obscured.

At this point it will be convenient to examine the popular traditional Catholic notion that the authority of the Scriptures is subordinate to that of the voice of the Church since the Scriptures arose out of the Church and were ratified by the Church, so that it is even alleged that the ordinary believer accepts the Scriptures as the Word of God on the authority of the Church. Setting aside the merely pedagogic and quite untheological idea of authority which this notion presupposes, it throws into startling relief the misunderstanding of the nature of Apostolic Succession from which traditional Catholicism suffers. Luther has surely said the last word on this subject. He is commenting on Galatians i. 8, 'But though we, or an angel from heaven, preach any other gospel unto you than that which we have preached unto you, let him be accursed.' And he says:

'The sentence of Paul upon all false teachers ought to admonish us, that so many as think the Pope to be the judge of the Scriptures, are accursed: which thing the Popish schoolmen have wickedly taught, standing upon this ground: the Church hath allowed four gospels only, therefore there are but four: for if it had allowed more, there would have been more.

'Now seeing the Church might allow and receive

so many gospels as it would, therefore the Church is above the gospel.

'A goodly argument forsooth—I approve the Scripture, therefore I am above the Scripture. John the Baptist acknowledgeth and confesseth Christ, and pointed to Him as the Lamb of God, therefore he is above Christ. The Church approveth the Christian faith and doctrine, therefore the Church is above them.

'For the overthrow of this wicked and blasphemous doctrine, thou hast here a plain text like a thunderbolt, wherein Paul subjecteth both himself and an angel from heaven, and all others, doctors, teachers and masters whatsoever, to be under the authority of the Scriptures: for they ought not to be masters, judges and arbiters, but only witnesses, disciples and confessors of the Church, whether it be the Pope or Luther or Augustine or Paul or an angel from heaven. Neither ought any doctrine to be taught or heard in the Church, beside the pure Word of God, that is, the Holy Scripture: otherwise accursed be the teachers and hearers, together with their doctrine.'[1]

It is difficult to see how there can be any gainsaying that. It was in virtue of That to which the Apostles witnessed and not of the fact that it was the Apostles who witnessed that the Bible possesses its authority and is able to speak to us as the Word

[1] *Galatians* (ed. Fallowes), pp. 26–7. Cf. chapter viii of Vincent of Lerins, *Commonitorium*, where, fundamentally, the exegesis is the same.

of God. And because of this the Church has no guarantee, as Paul asserts in this passage 'like a thunderbolt', of being able to know the Truth of God or to speak it unless she brings herself, as the Apostles had to, to the 'flesh of Jesus', Whose true significance must be spiritually discerned in the Holy Ghost. 'God remains the Lord in His own House.'[1]

In a chapter which is of the greatest importance for the attempt of Reformed and traditional Catholic theologians in England to understand each other on the doctrine of the Church,[2] Hoskyns discusses the attitude of Ignatius, from whose teaching traditional Catholicism always claims to derive much of its support, to the episcopate from this point of view. First of all, he emphasizes that what linked Ignatius to the Apostles was that they shared a common relation to Christ. Faced as he was with the prospect of martyrdom, he felt his kinship with the Apostles because the very mark of an Apostle was that he was joined to Christ's flesh and blood, the Christ Who died upon the cross. 'Ignatius does not mean by this merely that the Apostles had seen Jesus and possessed reminiscences of His flesh. He means that they were Apostles because, through their historical relation

[1] Barth in *Zwischen den Zeiten* (1928), p. 291. Quoted by Visser t'Hooft, *Anglo-Catholicism and Orthodoxy* (S.C.M.), pp. 169–70.

[2] *The Fourth Gospel*, chapter vi, 'The Fourth Gospel in the Second Century'.

to Jesus, they were found superior to death and because their lives in the flesh had been bent to obedience to God.'[1] That is, through the witness of the Apostles, Ignatius was able to stand where they stood and know the Jesus Who poured out His soul unto death as they knew Him.[2] And it is from *this* point of view that Ignatius' confidence in bishops is to be explained.

'Ignatius is not concerned with ecclesiastical administration any more than he is concerned with some peculiar kind of developing ecclesiastical othodoxy. He is concerned with the Church's apprehension of its mission, and consequently, with the preservation of the historical figure of Jesus. *It is in this context, and only in this context, that the ministry of the Church gains any significance at all*.[3] Ignatius speaks of bishops, not as though they were persons exercising some strange kind of independent mystical authority . . . but as men responsible for the preservation of the apostolic witness to Jesus. . . . Obedience to authority, no doubt, has in itself at all times theological and moral significance; but it is not for this reason that Ignatius demands obedience to bishops. He requires obedience to the bishops and the body of the elders in order that the Churches may be confirmed in the "ordinances of the Lord and of the

---

[1] Ibid., p. 114.

[2] The same point is well made in a wider context by Ramsey, *The Gospel of the Catholic Church*, pp. 48–9.

[3] Italics mine.

Apostles"; in order that Christians may be subject to the "Law of Jesus Christ and to the grace of God" . . . [an] administrative tyranny is precisely what Ignatius will not allow. He is concerned neither with administration nor with blind obedience to a bishop. . . . Bishops are to be heard only because they speak "concerning Jesus Christ in truth" and because there can be no "bread of God" apart from the sanctuary of obedience.'[1]

Thus here again, even when the authority of the Church in the persons of its bishops is asserted in the strongest possible way, it is only to make clear that the Church lives not from herself but from her Lord and that the Apostles are to be held in reverence just because and only because they are the witnesses, both with their words and their lives, to Jesus Christ, God's word.

The disastrous results of an inability to understand the precise relation of the Apostles to their Lord is shown by the following extraordinary quotation from Professor Clement Rogers. Admittedly, most responsible Anglo-Catholics would reject this position—which goes further even than the Roman claim, which is, after all, only to an infallible definition of the Gospel given in the Scriptures—as indignantly as we do, but it at least throws into relief the dangers of this approach.

'So again, as there are classics of the world's literature, there are also classics of religious writing

[1] *The Fourth Gospel*, pp. 115–17. Cf. also Ramsey, pp. 78–9.

which may be called Catholic. First of all, and pre-eminently, the Bible is the Book of the Church, especially when read or heard by the people in public worship. So it was that the books of the New Testament were collected and the canon formed. Some of those which were read Sunday by Sunday were found to be different from others. It was their universal appeal which marked them off. The Church existed before the Bible and the New Testament was written for the Church by the men of the Church. Its difference from other books was later accounted for by a theory of inspiration, but it was the practical Catholic test, *quod ab omnibus*, that separated the so inspired books.'[1]

And he goes on to describe the Christian classics of devotion and hymns and prayer as possessing the same character as the Bible for the same reasons. Is it a complete caricature of this position to assert that Professor Rogers might just as well say that God was a good idea which the Church had and which many people liked very much? Of course, the Bible was written by the Church for the Church, but only to make clear once and for all to the Church that she draws her life not from herself but from the living God in Jesus Christ Who always stands over against her in judgement and in promise. This is a secular Catholicism which starts from a preconceived notion of catholicity

[1] *A Church Genuinely Catholic* (S.P.C.K., 1940), pp. 164–5.

and adjusts the Scriptures to that. It is not the Catholicism of the *apostolic* Church.

All this, of course, in no way denies the genuine relative authority which Church tradition has in interpreting the apostolic testimony. The very fact that the Scriptures need exegesis demands such an authority and we can refuse to recognize it only by refusing to admit that the Spirit has been at work in the Church before us, that is, that the Church of our Fathers has been a true Church and our own Baptism a true Baptism. The crude appeal to the letter of the Scriptures, with no attention to the experience of the Spirit-guided Church, means not only a woeful impoverishment of the Church's life and worship. It frequently means also a crabbed and narrow interpretation of the Scriptures. The churchmanship of such bodies as the Strict Baptists and the Plymouth Brethren is sufficient proof of this. And there is no doubt that as against debased modern Protestantism, both of the Right and of the Left,[1] traditional Catholicism, in England especially, is performing a true service to catholicity by its emphasis on the importance of tradition. The question is, however, what it means by tradition. The Roman position is clear and, as we shall seek to show in detail later, by claiming to

[1] 'Why', asked P. T. Forsyth of modern Congregationalists, 'has [the idea of the authority of the Church] sunk to the rude political arbitrament of a living majority, when the real spiritual majority are the dead?' *The Principle of Authority* (Hodder & Stoughton), p. 11.

give an infallible definition of the nature of the apostolic testimony seems to us to deny the nature of that testimony by usurping a function which the Lord has reserved for Himself. But is that necessarily the position of non-Roman Catholicism of the Anglican type? We are unable to discover a conclusive answer. Mr. Eric Graham, in a very reasonable article in the volume, *Union of Christendom*,[1] says nothing with which a Reformed churchman could not agree. He says nothing more than can be comprehended, as Barth says, under obedience to the Fifth Commandment, 'Honour thy father and thy mother'.[2] And the same, as far as we can gather, is true of Ramsey.[3] Yet the tenacity with which Catholic Anglicans cling to a 'series' theory of Apostolic Succession seems to presuppose a belief that the living Word of the apostolic testimony is not ultimately sufficient but that 'the witness of the Church as given in tradition' is 'equally authoritative with the Bible itself'.[4] We must wait for the Church of England to clarify its position further on this point. For our part, it is enough at this stage to make clear, as indeed the whole of our fourth chapter will try to prove, that

[1] The Appeal to Scripture and Tradition, *Union of Christendom* (ed. McKenzie, S.P.C.K., 1938), pp. 549–72.

[2] *Credo* (Hodder & Stoughton), p. 181.

[3] And cf. Article VI and the Lambeth Quadrilateral.

[4] Report of Edinburgh Conference on Faith and Order, 1937, p. 9.

we readily accept the authority of tradition in so far as it is founded on Scripture and equally readily admit that modern Protestantism, and to some extent traditional Protestantism, has not been sufficiently mindful of that authority.

III

What, then, are the marks of primary catholicity, that quality which makes the Church to be the Church? We are in a position now to understand the significance of Barth's answer to this question. Reminding us that the distinction between a true and a false church cannot be drawn by us but can only be recognized by us in faith as one already made by God Himself, he goes on to say:

'Let a man ask . . . where there is to be found true preaching of the Word of God as witnessed to by the prophets and Apostles. Secondly, where are the sacraments as instituted by Jesus Christ rightly administered? Thirdly, where is to be found the ordinance of the Church, which is required of us by the Word of God and which means the necessary crisis also among individual men within the Church? Note that all these three points —these *notae ecclesiae*—are of a spiritual nature. All three say, the true church is to be seen where the Holy Spirit of God wills it. For God's Holy Spirit decides where there is true preaching, right administration of the sacraments and faithful accomplishment of this discipline and crisis. And *in what way* God's Holy Spirit decides in these matters, will be seen and known and recognized through faith and so through the Holy Spirit Himself. But God's Holy Spirit speaks and may be heard at the place where He has His dwelling and from which He comes to us, namely, in Jesus Christ as the Word of God. What the Reformed Confession means by specifying these three points is that, when we inquire about the true church and consider preaching, the sacraments and the ordinance of the church, it is Jesus Christ Himself as the Word of God, Who has to be the subject of our enquiry.'[1]

The presence of the Word and Sacraments and the ordinance of God in the form of the Church are thus the primary marks of catholicity, but it is vitally important that we should understand the exact sense in which this is true. The significant sentence in our quotation from Barth is: 'It is Jesus Christ Himself as the Word of God, Who has to be the subject of our enquiry.' That is, it is only in so far as the Word and the Sacraments and the pattern of life which they create for the Church are consciously brought ever and anew under the scrutiny of Jesus Christ, the living Word, as testified to by the Apostles, in order that the Church may ensure that she is, in fact, making manifest His Lordship and not usurping it, that

[1] *The Knowledge of God and the Service of God*, pp. 171–2. Cf. Calvin, *Institutio*, 4, i, 9, and the significant development in Barth.

they can be said to be the true marks of the Church. In that sense we may say that the ordinance of the Church, the bringing of her members under the discipline and crisis of the Word of God, of which we shall have more to say shortly, is the condition of the true preaching of the Word and the faithful dispensation of the Sacraments, while being itself impossible without the Word and Sacraments. The apparent argument in a circle is inevitable just because it is Jesus Christ, Who cannot be trapped in any human categories, Who is the subject of our inquiry. It is profoundly true that, as Calvin says, any congregation, no matter how unworthy its members may be, which possesses and honours 'the ministry of the Word, and the administration of the sacraments' is 'without all doubt entitled to be considered as a Church because it is certain that the Word and sacraments cannot be unattended with some good effects',[1] but nevertheless the Word and Sacraments can neither properly function in themselves nor reach their appointed goal unless they themselves and the whole life of the Church they create are brought under the κρίσις of the Word of God, Jesus Christ.

This brings us to the doctrine of Reformation according to the Word of God which is the nerve-centre of the Reformed doctrine of the Church but which, as far as we know, has never been systematically expounded, and until it was recently restated by Barth has been as frequently misunder-

[1] *Institutio*, 4, i, 9, Allen's translation, ii, p. 231.

stood by the 'Reformed' Churches themselves as it has been by the 'Catholic' Churches. Reformation according to the Word of God is a constant activity in the Church because it alone ensures that the Church continues to exist as the true Church and does not lapse into being a false church. The Church, as we have seen, is the Church only in so far as she gives heed to the Apostles' testimony, only, that is, in so far as she brings herself into subjection to the Word of God in Jesus Christ, and, by losing herself in witnessing to Him, makes manifest His Lordship. But the Church exists in this fallen world and is, therefore, always confronted with the possibility of becoming a false church. And just as, in this world, faith, existing in a constant tension with unbelief, is a series of constantly repeated acts of repentance—of turning back from self to God and acknowledging His Lordship in judgement, forgiveness, and newness of life—so also is the life of the Church on earth a series of constantly repeated acts of public repentance, of examining herself critically under the Word of God and of re-forming herself ever and anew in the light of that Word. It is to this truth, as we shall see later, that the whole rhythm of Divine Service is meant to testify, as Barth's Gifford lectures make clear. Where the so-called 'Reformed' Churches have gone wrong has been in imagining that because they are the 'lineal descendants' of the Reformers of the sixteenth and seventeenth centuries they need reform themselves no more, that they are now reformed, whereas, in point of fact, the Church is never reformed but is always in process of reformation. They have, in fact, fallen into precisely the same error as traditional Catholicism.[1] They imagine that they hold the Word as a secure possession which guarantees them their catholicity, so that they can now take for granted their existence as the Church. But the truth is that we hold the Word, Jesus Christ, only in faith, which means self-examination to ensure that we have not set up an idol in His place, and bringing ourselves into subjection to Him, that His Lordship, and therefore his Life, might be made manifest in us, since faith is the work of the Holy Spirit Who is His personal presence in us. Once again, as Barth says:

'The true Church, i.e. the reformed church, is always undergoing this reformation, this reformation, that is, of her preaching, her sacraments and her ordinance by the Word of God. The false church, that is always the unreformed church, was perhaps reformed four hundred years ago, only

[1] Cf. a paper by Pastor J. le Saussure on 'The Interrelation of Theology and (Secular) Knowledge' in *Proceedings of the Calvinistic Congress*, Edinburgh, 1938, pp. 205–36, in which 'Closed Calvinism', which finds in 'the systematized thought of Calvin the adequate and, consequently, immutable, expression of his doctrine' is shown to be a denial of the true Reformed position which regards faith as the only organ of dogmatic thought and therefore insists on the constant criticism of all systems in the light of the Word of God.

now to reveal the fact that she is afraid of allowing herself to be further reformed. Faith is necessary, that the Church may again and again undergo this reformation by the Word of God, and thus let herself be distinguished as the true Church from the false. And faith is necessary in order to see this distinction. What is divine will be done only by God. And that God does what is divine will only be known through God revealing it. . . .'[1]

It is this constant reforming action on the Church's part, then, whereby she acknowledges ever and anew that she belongs to Christ and not to any worldly sovereign and lives from Him alone that ensures that her Word and Sacraments and ordinance are truly His and thus reveal her as a true Church and not a false. In this sense it is the simple truth to say that only a reformed Church can hope to be the Catholic Church.

It is important, however, to specify more precisely what is involved in this act of reformation, as from it springs our understanding of the real test of catholicity. Firstly, it will be clear from our previous argument that, since it is the character of her witness which decides whether the Church stands in the succession of the Apostles, it will be the quality of her *proclamation* which will be the primary test of the Church's catholicity. This, of course, includes both Word and Sacraments, since both are part of the action of proclamation and

[1] *The Knowledge of God and the Service of God*, pp. 172–3.

51

cannot be separated without obscuring its true nature. As the indispensable instrument, therefore, by which the Church brings herself into subjection to the Lord she must constantly be asking herself, 'Is my preaching in fact the apostolic preaching?'[1] This she does by reference to the Scriptures, but not, as we have seen, simply by the method of historical verification, necessary though that is, but by listening to Jesus Christ, God's Word, Whose voice sounds through the Scriptures. And further, since in true preaching Jesus Christ becomes our contemporary and speaks to our condition in the voice of the preacher, the Church must not only discern the Word in the Scriptures and bring out its meaning against the background of the Scriptures but also, while paying heed to the light thrown upon its meaning in the history of the Church, state it anew in such a way that we can recognize it as the voice of our Lord, speaking as He spoke to the Apostles. That is to say, the Church, if she wishes to be a true Church, must pursue ceaselessly the task of critical Dogmatics. 'Theology', says Barth, 'and dogmatics in particular is, in contradistinction to all scattered answers to immaterial questions, the Church's concentrated anxiety and concern about her most intimate responsibility.'[2] We shall try to deal in

---

[1] By 'preaching' is meant here, of course, the whole of the Church's proclamation of her Lord, as well as, although especially, the sermons of her ministers.

[2] *Doctrine of the Word of God*, p. 84.

the next chapter with the exact sense in which Reformed theology conceives itself to be Catholic theology, but here we must underline the originality of this conception of the nature of Dogmatics as it has been so notably expounded by Barth in the Prolegomena to his great *Dogmatic* and its direct significance for the question of the nature of catholicity. The popular distinction between 'Historical' and 'Speculative' theology, reflected in the arrangement of courses in so many modern universities, in England, shows a complete misunderstanding of the function of theology in the Church. Dogmatics is not a free exercise of the human intellect. It is the indispensable servant of preaching, preaching which is the making manifest of God's Lordship in Christ ever and anew in the Church. Once again, Barth says, 'As a theological discipline, dogmatics is the scientific test to which the Christian Church puts herself regarding the language about God which is peculiar to her.'[1] And as its subject-matter is Jesus Christ, the content of the apostolic testimony, its method is the leading of the mind of the Church away from 'the wisdom of words' to the 'cross of Christ'. Dogmatics can, therefore, be spoken of as the Church's repentance, her acknowledgement of her Lord in her proclamation, and where it is not pursued with the most thorough and prayerful devotion the Church's proclamation is imperilled and the Church's life poisoned at the springs. This is

[1] *Doctrine of the Word of God*, p. 1.

clearly true of the Church's preaching, but we must insist that it is no less true of her Sacraments. Certainly, the effect of Christ's ordinance is not taken away by the wickedness of its ministers,[1] but it is if the Church makes no attempt to ensure that it is administered according to Christ's 'institution and promise' and that attempt is the work of critical Dogmatics. The quality of a Church's theological faculties, therefore, is a far more sure indication of her catholicity than the quality of her pedigree.

Secondly, the Church must also bring her form in the world under the discipline and κρίσις of the Word of God. The Church's proclamation does not exist in a vacuum but must express itself in the form of the Church's life. Modern Protestantism has so far forgotten this fact that Ramsey's claim that Church Order is an expression of the Gospel comes to it with a shock of surprise, but it was this which really lay behind the concern of the Calvinist fathers for the godly discipline. They conceived of it in too external a way, so that it ended by becoming a tyranny of the consistory with a sectarian, negative, and moralistic conception of the 'discipline', but in the beginning it was a useful reminder that the Word and Sacraments do not make manifest God's Lordship unless the Church hears Christ speaking in them and obeys His voice.[2] The ordinance of the Church, which

[1] Article **XXVI** of the **XXXIX** Articles.
[2] Cf. Ramsey, p. 125: 'The Church's work in thinking

is perhaps a better phrase than the 'godly discipline' of unfortunate associations, is the inevitable issue of the Church's repentance in proclamation, critical Dogmatics. The Church's worship, her Ministry, her education, her attitude to the common life should all exist as means whereby the Church turns away from the 'form of this world' and fashions herself 'according to its transformation', being transformed by that 'renewing of her mind', that bringing of herself into subjection to the Word of God and making manifest in these spheres His Lordship, which is the function of her proclamation. Thus this is pre-eminently true of the Church's worship, as we shall try to show in greater detail later. And perhaps it is useful to remind ourselves to-day, when we are learning a new respect for the forms of traditional Catholic worship, that it was this kind of truly catholic reforming zeal which was behind the Protestant reform of worship in the sixteenth and seventeenth centuries. The function of public worship is to turn men away from themselves and all outward forms to the glory of God in the face of Jesus Christ. This is worship 'in Spirit and in truth' of the God Who is a Spirit, and interpreting and teaching is inseparable from the Church's life in Christ. Its authority is Christ Himself, known in the building up of the one Body in Truth and in Love. Hence "orthodoxy" means not only "right opinion", but also "right worship" or "true glory", after the Biblical meaning of the word $\delta\delta\xi a$; for life and thought and worship are inseparable activities in the Body of Christ.'

not in the sense of Quakerism and the 'Spiritualizers', with their lamentable tendency to lapse into
mere subjectivism and hence a monologue of the
soul with itself, but in the sense of God Who by
speaking in His Word, Jesus Christ, has already
shown His preference for the spiritual rather than
the material as a vehicle of revelation.[1] It was this
impulse which made the Puritans react so violently
against images and elaborate ceremonial. We have
reason to regret the thoughtlessness with which
the reformation was frequently carried out and the
lack of discrimination, and in the later stages the
downright Philistinism, with which they failed to
distinguish between seemly traditional observance
and pompous or irrelevant show, but we can at
least understand sympathetically that their zeal did
represent a genuine attempt to reform the ordinance of the Church according to the Word of
God.[2] That this movement of reformation in the

[1] Cf. Barth on 'the relative canonization of the spiritual'
in *The Doctrine of the Word of God*, p. 152.
[2] And we are bound to wonder whether the need for
this particular kind of witness has altogether passed away
when we read, 'We believe Divine over-ruling so shaped
the course of the English Reformation as to ensure that
"Northern Catholicism" should find a home and a concrete embodiment, not in mere individual pamphleteering
nor in any obscure and self-centred sect, but in a great
and venerable Church, historically linked with the life of
a famous nation, endowed with a magnificent array of
cathedral and parish churches, which include some of the
greatest temples of the Christian world, and preserving in

dynamic sense we have attempted to give it must be present is most clear, then, in the Church's worship, but it must be no less present in all our 'Christian walk and conversation' as well. The way in which the Church conceives the nature of her Ministry and the way in which she conceives her relation to the world and her task in the world, a question of which we are barely on the fringe in any serious sense, must also come under the judgement of the Word of God. In all these spheres, sinful human nature is attempting to assert itself against God and thus to turn the Church into a false church. And in order to ensure that she remains catholic the Church must constantly be scrutinizing all these forms of her life in the light of God's Word and bringing them into subjection to Him. What this involves we shall try to elaborate in the succeeding chapters.

them a tradition of public and solemn liturgical observance which is the envy of many less-favoured parts of Christendom.' (N. P. Williams, *Northern Catholicism*, Foreword, pp. xiv–xv). Cf. Isaiah i. 10–17 and liii. 2 and Philippians iii. 8.

Chapter III

THE BURDEN OF THE APOSTOLIC
TESTIMONY: JESUS CHRIST

I

In the last chapter we discovered that the marks of catholicity are the possession of Jesus Christ as He is known through the apostolic testimony in the Word and the Sacraments and the bringing of the form of the Church under the judgement of Jesus Christ that His Lordship might be made manifest in it. In this chapter we shall endeavour to define the way in which the presence of Jesus Christ in the Church guarantees to her her catholicity, and in the next we shall try to examine the nature of the Catholic Christian and the form of the Catholic Church, created by and witnessing to His Lordship.

Ubi Christus, ibi ecclesia. Once again we state the fundamental principle of catholicity, but it is in this context more, perhaps, than in any other that its implications are not clearly seen. It is extraordinary how uncatholic, in the sense of failing to keep the 'proportion of faith' (T. A. Lacey) but concentrating on secondary considerations, traditional Catholicism is in defining the marks of catholicity. Its exponents have, apparently, failed to see, although, of course, this is the inwardness of their own official doctrine, that, in the words of Barth already quoted, 'it is Jesus Christ Himself as the Word of God, Who has to be the subject of our enquiry'.[1] Generally they have contented themselves with explaining why communion with the see of Rome or historical succession through the laying on of hands by the monarchical episcopate or fulfilment of the Vincentian Canon, as the case may be, is essential to catholicity without defining the way in which these things are related to the knowledge of Jesus Christ by which they are alone justified.

Why, then, is the presence of Jesus Christ alone the primary mark of the Church's catholicity? The answer lies at the heart of the Christological dogma. Because He alone is truly God and truly man. The Chalcedonian Definition, on which traditional Catholicism rightly lays such stress, demands as its logical fulfilment the Catholicism of the Word and the principle of Reformation according to the Word of God! It is the foundation of the Christian faith and therefore of the Church that Jesus Christ is God. In the earliest records we have it was the confession 'Jesus is Lord' at baptism which was taken as proof that converts were now ready for

[1] Father Congar, O.P., in his *Divided Christendom* (English translation, Centenary Press), is a striking exception.

admission to membership of the Church.[1] If, then, Jesus Christ is God, where Jesus Christ dwells God in all His fullness dwells. 'And in Him', says Colossians in the strongest possible manner, 'dwelleth all the fullness of the Godhead bodily'.[2] But in God, Who by His very nature is the ultimate Reality, the fullness of the truth must dwell. His sovereignty is a universal sovereignty and holds throughout all space and time and beyond it. Where God is, and therefore where Jesus Christ is, there can be nothing which does not depend for its existence and for its reality upon Him. 'All things were made by Him and without Him was not any thing made that hath been made.'[3] In God there can be nothing relative or temporary or ambiguous, and hence no half-truths, no sectarianism, no provincialism, no obscurantism. It is manifestly absurd, therefore, as men in all ages but especially in modern Europe appear to have forgotten, for man, however wise or experienced or 'free-thinking' or self-conscious or realistic or disillusioned he may be, to put questions to God

---

[1] It is perhaps necessary to point out as against those who, on the basis of this fact would make any kind of 'love' for Jesus Christ, whether as Lord or 'Leader', the condition of membership of the Church that the word 'Lord' is undoubtedly used here against the background of the Old Testament. He is therefore Very God of Very God in the most absolute sense and the truth of the doctrine of the Two Natures is already implicit in the Baptismal Confession.

[2] Col. ii. 9.   [3] John i. 3.

of which He does not know the answer, as though there were some levels of reality beyond the ken of the ultimate Reality. All our human conceptions are relative and limited, just because they are human. Even our conception of the Absolute is such and our salvation consists in our willingness to recognize and accept this fact. But God, and He alone, is truly absolute and unlimited, truly personal and truly free, deriving His essence and His existence from Himself, complete, ultimate, self-sufficing. As Barth puts it:

'The human idea of the Absolute, which we are accustomed to think of as identical with God, is the reflection of the world, and in the end the disastrous reflection of human personality. Once again, if we had equated this idea with God, we would have set up the image of an idol. We have not to draw our knowledge of who God is from what we think we know about eternity, infinity, omnipotence and invisibility as conceptions which bound our thought. On the contrary, we have to draw our knowledge of eternity, infinity, omnipotence and invisibility from what we can know about God, from what God has said to us about Himself.'[1]

And because Jesus Christ is what God has said to us about Himself, when we know Jesus Christ we know the fullness of truth and the whole universe holds no more decisive secret from us.

[1] *The Knowledge of God and the Service of God*, pp. 32–3. This is elaborated in the second volume of the *Dogmatic*.

Jesus Christ is Very God, but Jesus Christ is also very man, and it is here that the sense in which His presence is the mark of the Church's catholicity emerges most directly. The passage in Colossians we have already quoted goes on to say, 'And in him ye are made full, who is the head of all principality and power.'[1] Once again the development of the Two Natures doctrine serves to give us clear guidance. Jesus Christ did not, as the Nestorian heresy implied, assume a particular human personality, in the sense of a unique centre of responsible existence.[2] If that had happened He would have been a relative, finite, temporally conditioned unit of the human race with a life and work of no more ultimate significance, however enduring their effect on history might be before it faded away, than that of anyone else. For, as Barth puts it once again, 'God is a Person in a way quite different from that in which we are persons. Our relation to others conditions what we are. Our existence as persons requires a world around us with the conditions and limitation which such a world imposes.'[3] But Jesus Christ, in becoming man, retains His divine personal existence, as indeed He had to if He was to remain Himself, and it is inconceivable that He could ever cease to be Himself. He becomes, therefore, not *a* man

[1] Col. ii. 10.
[2] Cf. E. Brunner, *The Mediator* (Lutterworth Press), chapter xiii.
[3] *The Knowledge of God and the Service of God*, p. 31.

but man. The Scriptures say that the Word became flesh, not that God became a man. He assumes human nature, that which is essential to the manhood we all share while each remaining distinct and individual persons. And by thus assuming manhood He becomes the archetypal man, the Second Adam, so that, through His standing where we stand and bearing the burden of our sin and His overcoming of it in His resurrection and exaltation, He restores to us our true humanity which we had lost by our rebellion against God. We are able to find our true humanity only in relation to God Who made us, only when He looks upon us as His children and we reflect His glory, and this can happen to us only in so far as we are in Jesus Christ, for, through His assumption of our humanity, God now looks upon us as we are in Him, His beloved Son in Whom He is well pleased. Apart from Him we cannot attain either to the truth about our nature or to the fullness of our manhood. Apart from Him we misconceive all that we are meant to be, becoming distorted, restless creatures, over-emphasizing now one side of ourselves and now another, given to over-optimism or over-pessimism in our view of life according to our lot and temperament, constantly at odds with our fellows but never finding true stability and fulfilment. The Bible, of course, insists that it is only by our incorporation into Jesus Christ, only by becoming members of His Body, that the essence and the fullness of manhood can be achieved. 'For of His fulness we all received, and grace for grace.'[1] But the most significant passage is the great section in the fourth chapter of Ephesians,[2] which is the classic text for the doctrine of catholicity as it refers to the fullness of the Church. The Apostle begins by reminding his readers of the unity of the Church which is based upon the Unity of God the Father, Whose Lordship controls all and pervades all and sustains all. Office in the Church, the Ministry in all its forms, is the gift of the ascended Christ and the result, as he points out in an aside, not of any distinctive virtue of the ministers, but of Christ's humiliation and exaltation, and office is given for 'the building up of the body of Christ' until 'we all attain unto the unity of the faith, and of the knowledge of the Son of God, unto the measure of the stature of the fulness of Christ' which is, and this is our point, the same as attaining 'unto a full-grown man'. When that happens, we are 'no longer children tossed to and fro and carried about with every wind of doctrine, by the sleight of men, in craftiness, after the wiles of error, but speaking the truth in love', we 'grow up in all things into him, which is the head, even Christ'. And that means that all the parts of our being fall into their proper place and perform their true function so that in our relations with each other we can manifest the unity of the Body which depends upon the unity of the most holy Trinity. 'From whom all the body fitly

[1] John i. 16.   [2] Ephesians iv. 4–16.

framed and knitted together through that which every joint supplieth, according to the working in due measure of each several part, maketh the increase of the body unto the building up of itself in love.'

It is necessary, however, to interject here that this 'attaining unto a full-grown man' is the same as the work of Christ in us, the restoration of the image of God which we had lost through our sin. This doctrine implies no kind of continuity between the 'old man' and the 'new man in Christ' and therefore no kind of naturalistic basis for the Church and no kind of anthropological or sociological or geographical definition of catholicity.[1] Nor is this the picture of Christ as the perfect example and inspiration for the attainment of fully rounded personality, 'the Secret of Victorious Living', such as Liberalism might provide.

It is because Jesus Christ became man, then, that His presence guarantees to us that we are in possession of the fullness of the truth as it concerns our existence as men, just as His Divinity guarantees to us that His truth is universally valid. The purpose of man's existence is to make manifest God's own glory. The creation is under a debt of gratitude to its Creator and since it is man who is addressed in revelation man has been called by the Creator to present the gratitude of the creation

[1] As in Professor Clement Rogers' *A Church Genuinely Catholic.*

E 65

to Himself.[1] It is in Jesus Christ and His resurrection and His return to His Father, bearing with Him the first-fruits of the new creation, that that purpose is fulfilled and nowhere else. All lapses from the fullness of catholic truth are due to the failure of men to see that and their believing that the universe somewhere holds a deeper and more abiding truth and, therefore, a more real mode of existence than that which is to be found in Jesus Christ. This is the reason, for example, for the well-known sense of inferiority of 'Modernist' theologians in the presence of what they call 'modern thought' and, equally, for the inferiority complex of 'Fundamentalist' theologians in the presence of Biblical Criticism. Indeed, all attempts at justifying God's self-revelation by criteria other than those which the revelation itself provides are due to an inadequate understanding of what is involved in the resurrection of Jesus Christ. The cosmic significance of the resurrection is that the Devil's attempt to assert his own sovereignty in the universe, that is, to set himself up as the centre of all reality and of catholic truth, has been defeated. God has shown Himself to be the absolute Master of the Devil, so that in His presence the Devil's 'truth' is seen to be not merely provincial and obscurantist—that is the case with the 'truth' of the philosophers who, after all, cannot be identified with the Devil—but also a lie.

[1] Barth, *The Knowledge of God and the Service of God*, p. 41. Cf. Rom. viii. 19–23.

The surest test, therefore, of a Church's claim to catholicity is whether its preaching, like the apostolic preaching, proclaims as its central message the resurrection from the dead of Jesus Christ, 'whom God raised up, having loosed the pangs of death, because it was not possible that he should be holden of it'.[1] This is the heart of true Reformed preaching and the pivot of Reformed theology and the justification of its claim that its theological method is the only possible one for truly catholic theology. Perhaps, as we have already hinted, the exact sense in which Reformed theology conceives itself to be the catholic theology has never been sufficiently defined. This is partly due to the fact that the Reformers in the sixteenth century do not appear to have been fully conscious themselves of the exact nature of the theological method which they in fact used nor to have appreciated fully its originality and the essential place which it must have in the life of the Church. There is no doubt that this is one of the chief causes of the partial failure of seventeenth-century theology and the complete failure of theology in later centuries to understand the presuppositions which must govern theological activity in the Reformed Churches. The result is that to-day, in England particularly, Reformed theology is always being misunderstood in terms of something else. Practically all the criticism of Barth which is heard in England, for example, is from the point of view of Reformed

[1] Acts ii. 24.

67

theology itself entirely irrelevant, because the critics show no sign of understanding the terms of reference which he uses. The Reformed theologian —and Barth is the Reformed theologian *par excellence*—is concerned only to make manifest the fullness of God's revelation of Himself in Jesus Christ, Very God and Very Man, as the Lord over all our life, and to expose all the attempts which men ceaselessly make, whether wittingly or unwittingly, to interpret that revelation in such a way as to deny His Lordship. To criticize this theology, therefore, because it does not do justice, according to the critics, to the sentiments of 'modern man' or recognize as equally valid with the Self-revelation in Jesus Christ the findings which they claim to have reached about God and man through philosophy or psychology or anthropology or comparative religion or pastoral work is simply to declare that the whole purpose of the theology has been misunderstood. It is to be unaware of the radical criticism which it passes on all the presuppositions with which its critic is unconsciously working. The Reformed theologian fixes his eye on Jesus Christ and tries never to waver from Him, and since, as we have tried to show, the presence of Jesus Christ in the Church is the mark of its catholicity, he can reasonably claim that, however imperfect his own use of it must necessarily be, his method is the only possible catholic method.

It is perhaps in this context that the reason for the fierce antipathy of Reformed theology to

Natural Theology is best understood. The Reformed attack on Natural Theology is due to an anxiety to preserve the catholicity of the Church because a preoccupation with Natural Theology involves a turning away from Jesus Christ Who is the life of the Church. Natural Theology attempts to set up another source of knowledge of God alongside Jesus Christ and thus threatens His Lordship. It immediately plunges us, however much it may speak of a *philosophia perennis*, into the sphere of the relative and the contingent, of half-truths and half-lies, of heresy, the great enemy of catholicity, which gives rise to parties and sects and all the harshness of fanaticism which prevent us keeping 'the unity of the Spirit in the bond of peace'. This can be illustrated historically from the way in which Roman Catholicism, which in ethics has leant heavily on the idea of Natural Law, the ally of Natural Theology, has articulated itself in terms of a very sharply defined sociological structure which it is driven to defend—as the reading of the popular Catholic press and a study of the methods used by certain Catholic apologists makes only too clear—by precisely that technique of 'propaganda' which modern politicians use in order to persuade people that a relative truth is really an absolute one, and which is the exact opposite of the 'witness' of the true Christian, his readiness to let the Truth speak for Itself, his 'demonstration of the Spirit and of power'. And it is significant that the more fully traditional

Catholicism develops along its own lines the more it emphasizes the importance of Natural Theology and Natural Law and the more it reveals the bigotry and arrogance and one-sidedness of heresy. Thus this tendency manifests itself much less clearly in English Catholicism, which is in a largely undeveloped state and owes some kind of vague allegiance to the principle of Reformation according to the Word of God,[1] than it does in Roman Catholicism.

Something similar happens when the Vincentian Canon is abstracted from its context and used, without reference to the conditions which governed its use in the intention of Saint Vincent, as an infallible criterion of catholicity. We do not dispute the helpfulness of the Canon in its proper place as a convenient rule of thumb for finding out how much authority a new doctrine can claim for itself, and we shall admit freely that modern Protestantism would be the better for its more frequent use, but it holds all the value it possesses relatively to the Scriptures, which are the testimony of the Apostles themselves. This was what Saint Vincent himself, despite several expressions which read ambiguously in the light of later developments, obviously intended.[2] But when the use of the Canon is not controlled by the Scriptures, then it can be easily manipulated to suit the prejudices of partisans and to avoid bringing Church proclama-

[1] The reference is to Article VI.
[2] Cf. *Commonitorium*, chapter xxviii, § 71.

tion under the Word of God in Jesus Christ. He alone is infallible and the Church which lives by Him but is always open to the possibility of falling away from Him, no matter how many safeguards it takes, can and does err. And at best the authority which the most diligent and honest use of the Canon can provide is only a rough, approximate, this-worldly authority. It is impossible, in the strictest sense, to say exactly what has been believed *semper, ubique, quem ab omnibus*. No-one can accept the use of the Vincentian Canon by itself as a satisfactory test of catholicity who takes the nature of divine authority seriously unless he claims that the voice of what he defines as the Church is, *simpliciter*, the voice of Christ. But that leads us on to the subject of our next section.

II

It is, then, because Jesus Christ is the Son of God, Who became man for our salvation, that His presence is the mark of the reality and the fullness of the Church. But while, as we have seen, Reformed theology protests that the preoccupation of traditional Catholicism with Natural Theology and Natural Law amounts to the setting up of another authority alongside Jesus Christ which challenges His Lordship, nevertheless all Churches would agree that, in some form or another, the Church's catholicity is ultimately derived from Jesus Christ.[1]

[1] Cf. the fine passage, 'Ecclesia in Christo', in Congar, *Divided Christendom*, pp. 60–3.

Where the conflict emerges in its sharpest and most significant form is in dealing with the relation in which the Church stands to Jesus Christ her Lord. Here Reformed theology, though it acknowledges in penitence that its principle has never been properly grasped by the Reformed Churches, is driven to stand in unshakable opposition to the characteristic teaching of traditional Catholicism. It agrees—and arising as it does out of the debased Churches of neo-Protestantism it agrees with exceptional readiness in these days—that the doctrine of traditional Catholicism is a serious attempt to insist on the reality of the visible Church as the redeemed Humanity and the minister of God's grace to the world, but it has to raise the question of whether, as Barth puts it in his unanswerable attack on the Catholic doctrine of Succession, what we have here is not so much a representation as a replacement of Christ.[1]

According to Reformed theology, the Church possesses Christ never as an assured possession which she is able to take for granted, as she does the external forms of her own life, but always in faith, always, that is, in such a way that Christ retains His sovereignty over her and in her. Possessing Christ in faith means possessing Him only in so far as the Church is *repentant*, only in so far as she is constantly turning from the form of this world and ever and anew acknowledging His

[1] *The Doctrine of the Word of God*, p. 109. The whole excursus, pp. 107–11, is of the first importance.

72

Lordship in her own life. 'Lord, I believe, help thou mine unbelief' is as much the prayer of the Church as of the individual believer. Christ exists in His Church not in such a way that He surrenders His Lordship to the Church, but in such a way that His Lordship is made manifest in all its freedom, so that the Church's proclamation of His Lordship is, not the means to her self-glorification, but her *service*. It is for this reason that, as Barth has reminded us, the Church's worship is rightly called the *service* of God. And as we shall go on to show, it is to this that the Church's Order is designed to testify. The Sacraments themselves are the most striking reminder that we thus walk by faith and not by sight, that we are strangers and sojourners upon the earth, so that when the Word becomes flesh for us we behold His glory only with the eye of faith, under the veils of the bread and the wine. The Feast as we know it on earth is not an extension into time of the Feast as it will be in Heaven. It is a temporary dispensation, a table prepared before us in the presence of our enemies, and it points us forward 'until He come' to the glory of the Feast in Heaven. Protagonists of the traditional Catholic doctrine of Succession sometimes try to defend it by claiming that the significant thing is not the bare fact of external historical connection but the continuity of sacramental life which the laying on of hands guarantees. But surely the whole point of the Sacraments is that they are the signs of the *mystery*, reminders

73

that God's grace will not permit itself to be externalized and canalized in this way. The continuity of sacramental life is precisely that which cannot be made the external mark of the Church's catholicity because the Sacraments bear testimony to what is, from our human side, the incalculability of God's action, to the fact that God retains His freedom in His revelation and that the life of the Church, the Communion of Saints, is 'hid with Christ in God'. Admittedly, the doctrine of transubstantiation, with its crass 'objectification'[1] and hence its depersonalization of Christ's presence, is able to link itself on intelligibly enough to this conception of historical succession as guaranteeing the continuity of sacramental life—once again the impressive unity and coherence of Roman Catholic Dogmatics as against that of English Catholicism is demonstrated—but the doctrine of transubstantiation is itself one of the points where the Roman Catholic misconception of the relation between Christ and His Church is most startlingly revealed.[2] In the same way, as we have already emphasized, the apostolic testimony is not one of the many graces which inhere in the Church's nature and need only to be developed properly by her, so that she can confidently assume that whenever she speaks she must necessarily speak in the accents of the Apostles. It is something which

[1] In the sense familiarized by Buber and Heim.
[2] Cf. Barth, *The Knowledge of God and the Service of God*, p. 200.

74

stands always over against the Church, as it did over against the persons of the Apostles themselves, and indeed this differentiation of the Gospel from the Church is essential for the Church's very existence, for it reminds her that she lives, not through some self-generating power of her own, but from God her Lord. This is a conception which well-disposed Catholics find difficult to grasp in all its ramifications,[1] but it is essential that it be made as clear as possible, for it is the crux of the whole discussion and unless we understand each other here no real progress can be made, however much we may imagine we are being drawn nearer each other.[2] As Visser t'Hooft puts it, 'They [speaking

---

[1] It is Congar's apparent inability to grasp this Reformed criticism of the Roman Catholic position which vitiates for us the argument of his otherwise admirable book. The decisive point for his whole argument is the identification which the Roman Church makes of the voice of the Church on earth with the voice of Christ. That identification is assumed throughout his book, it is not justified, and nowhere does he show any awareness of the Reformed criticism of it. So completely, indeed, does he misunderstand it that he is driven to allege (p. 91) that Protestantism denies the reality of the Incarnation, whereas, in fact, Protestantism asserts that it is Roman Catholicism which will not assume for itself 'the form of a servant' which has missed the true significance of the Incarnation.

[2] It does not augur well for ultimate re-union between traditional Catholic and Reformed Churches that delegates at the Edinburgh Conference on Faith and Order were able to find themselves with very little difficulty in complete agreement on the Theology of Grace!

75

particularly of non-Roman Catholics, but it holds, of course, even more strongly of Roman Catholics] are right in believing that God has spoken and speaks through the Church, but not in believing that therefore the voice of the Church is to be identified with the Word of God Himself. "For God remains the Lord of His own House" (Karl Barth). The agreement between God and His Church is never a point of departure but at best a point of arrival of Christian faith.'[1] And in order to arrive at this point, as we have also already tried to make clear, the Church has to undergo the critical activity of examining herself and her proclamation by Jesus Christ in the Scriptures and reforming her preaching and her life in the light of His scrutiny—the mutual relations of the Word, proclamation, Dogmatics and discipline thus helping us to understand the relation between Christ and His Church. And similarly, as t'Hooft goes on to say, 'If there is any continuity in the life of the Christian and in the life of the Church, it is not a continuity in time and space but a continuity of God's creative action. Sometimes God's continuity will seem to us an interruption in the human development. To Protestants the event of the Reformation is a strong case in point. They cannot see the action of Luther as an arbitrary break-away from a sacred tradition, for to them it represents the restoration of a deeper and invisible continuity

[1] *Anglo-Catholicism and Orthodoxy* (S.C.M., 1933), pp. 169–70.

in faith.'[1] And Barth has put the case against the Roman doctrine of Succession with decisive force.

'Is not the vicariate in the Roman sense a thing in which only the accidents of the vicariate are retained, while in substance it is simply the rule of Christ become identical with the rule of the Church? We realise that this whole doctrine is a truly significant attempt to come to terms with the problem of real proclamation. But does not this solution mean that proclamation (through the ideas of the historical succession, the *character indelibilis*, and the possibility of unalterable definitions) is dehumanised, i.e. drawn into a sphere in which it is only in appearance that it can signify a humanly assailable, responsible, surpassable and therefore serviceable action? It was certainly logical, but it is still a fact we face with discomposure, that on his consecration Innocent III preached simply— about himself (Harnack, *Christus praesens—Vicarius Christi*, p. 441). Even Roman Catholic Dogmatics is naturally aware that the Lordship of Christ is a lordship not only *in* His Church but *over* His Church. But where in this system can this lordship of Christ over His Church become *concrete*, where can it get its proper play, when a complete transfer of all its power to the Church has already taken place, when its power in the Church is simply *there*? And if it has no proper play, is it distinguished otherwise than merely by

[1] *Anglo-Catholicism and Orthodoxy*, p. 172.

name from the power exercised in the Church by men without break, let or limit?'[1]

In confirmation of this, if confirmation be needed, there is the passage in Newman[2] where we are told that, on the principle of the analogy of Natural and Revealed Religion, 'what conscience is in the system of nature, such is the voice of the Scriptures or of the Church or of the Holy See, as we may determine it, in the system of revelation'. In effect Scripture (it is interesting that he falls into the common Catholic error of imagining that Scripture has the same *kind* of authority for Protestants as the Church or the Holy See has for Catholics) or the Church or the Holy See—in this case the Holy See—is identical with the Holy Ghost since, as he goes on to make clear, 'when such external authority is taken away the mind falls back of necessity upon that inward guide it possessed even before Revelation was vouchsafed'. That is, if a man cannot hear the voice of the Holy See he cannot hear the voice of Christ, for there is no means whereby the voice can reach him except the Holy See, and therefore there can be no appeal from a pronouncement of the Holy See to Christ.

Where this distinction between the Church and her Lord is not clearly understood the Church inevitably, just because she exists in this fallen world and is ceaselessly open to the attacks of the

[1] *The Doctrine of the Word of God*, p. 109.
[2] *Essay on the Development of Doctrine*, pp. 85–7.

Devil, seeks to rob Christ of His Lordship and to set up in His place an idol of her own creation whom she worships as Christ. This, indeed, is the characteristic temptation of the Church, and the index of her catholicity is the extent of her awareness of this temptation and her vigilance in seeking to avoid it.[1] It is the presence of Jesus Christ Himself in the Spirit which alone ensures that the Church is a true Church, and whenever, as she is always in danger of doing, the Church allows herself to rest content with her possession of the tokens of revelation and does not allow them to perform their proper function of leading her beyond them to Christ Himself, then she is led astray. Thus even Creeds, Ministry, Scripture itself are not free from the danger of being turned from safeguards of the Gospel into hindrances of it. Each of them needs the quickening touch of Christ's living presence if they are not to be used as subtle means by which men can lull themselves into a false security concerning the safety of the Church's catholicity and thus allow the Devil to usurp Christ's throne. It is because of this possibility that we are compelled to question Ramsey's dictum, 'The structure of catholicism is an utterance of the Gospel'.[2] That the structure of Catholicism *witnesses* to the Gospel we do not deny, and

[1] In this sense it is not improper to speak of Barth's *Commentary on the Epistle to the Romans* as the first great work of the Catholic revival in modern Europe.
[2] *The Gospel and the Catholic Church*, p. 54.

we are grateful to Ramsey for reminding us of it with such force and clarity. And, because it witnesses to the Gospel, that it is the creation of the Gospel and in one sense the expression of the Gospel we also do not deny. But to say that it is an utterance of the Gospel *simpliciter* is to overlook this possibility that it may be exploited to mislead men rather than to lead them. It fulfils its function only when it points men to the living Christ. But to say that it is itself an utterance of the Gospel suggests that in itself it is the living Christ. Ramsey is himself conscious of the peril that, to use his own words, 'the devout churchman' may 'turn his religion into a "glory to me", "glory to this movement", "glory to the Church" religion instead of a "glory to God" religion',[1] but imagines that it is only the 'spiritualizers' against whom the historical facts of Christianity and 'the structure of the one Body' claiming continuity with them are an effective safeguard are open to this peril. He appears to be unaware of the dangers of 'legalizers' or the 'institutionalizers' who mistake the form of the Church for its reality, even though the purpose of the form is undoubtedly to point to the reality. We cannot believe that there will be ultimate disagreement between Reformed churchmen and Catholics of Ramsey's school on this point,[2] but as surely as they rightly insist on

[1] *The Gospel and the Catholic Church*, p. 56.

[2] Cf. Ramsey, p. 201, but his remarks on Barth on p. 203 make us wonder whether Catholicism is yet in a

the relation between Church Order and the Gospel as against Protestantism which has forgotten it, so we insist on the tension between the Gospel and Church Order which traditional Catholicism appears to have overlooked. It is in this sense only that we can understand the familiar traditional Catholic argument that Protestantism depends for its existence upon Catholicism, of which it is a criticism. What we must see, both traditional Catholics and Protestants, is that the criticism in the light of the Word of God is itself the only way in which the Church can make sure of its catholicity. Without the structure of Catholicism we are in danger of losing the fullness of the Church, but without the criticism of Protestantism, which we prefer to call reformation according to the Word of God, we are in danger of losing the essence of the Church.

There is some ground for saying that in the providence of God, those branches of the Church which have been careful to preserve 'the structure of catholicism' as they conceived it, notably a liturgy based on ancient forms, the monarchical episcopate and emphasis on the Oecumenical Creeds as doctrinal standards, have, speaking very generally, been enabled to maintain more of the marks of the Church than those branches which did not. This is most obviously true, perhaps, of the Church of England as contrasted with the position to 'face the issues of the Gospel and examine itself as to its Pelagianism'.

English 'Free' Churches. In so far as the English 'Free' Churches have retained the Scriptures as the centre of their life this does not apply, but where, as has happened in some cases, the authority of the Scriptures has been challenged or misunderstood, then the marks of the Church have almost entirely disappeared. Speaking against the background of modern Congregationalism in particular, we have to question the spiritual wisdom, to put it at its lowest, of our Fathers three hundred years ago in paying so little attention to the value of Liturgy, Ministry, and Creeds as pointers to the right understanding of the Word as it is in Scripture. We shall have much more to say about this in our next chapter. But we are bound in all humility and certainly without any feeling of self-satisfaction, for, as we freely admit, the 'Free' Churches have no particular cause for glorying in their own traditions in recent generations, to inquire whether history as well as the logic of theology does not bear out the truth that to place the essential mark of catholicity anywhere except in Jesus Christ, God's Word, known in judgement and in promise through the Scriptures and in all else only derivatively from the Scriptures, is not to corrupt the Church and to make her increasingly bigoted, complacent, and sectarian. For a Church to feel sure of its catholicity because of certain historical characteristics its ministry possesses or because of its liturgy or because it is in communion with other Churches which call themselves Catholic

—all of them external criteria within human control—is to lull itself into a sense of security the true Church does not know or desire to know on this earth and to excuse itself from undergoing that discipline and crisis through the Word of God which will alone give it catholicity. Its preaching is cut off from its roots and in the end is bound to wither and die. And in such circumstances, may not even a passionate devotion to the Sacrament mask a spiritual laziness which destroys the meaning of the Sacrament? And similarly, may not an unquestioning acceptance of 'traditional orthodoxy' as enshrined in the Creeds and formularies of the Church serve as an excuse not merely for stifling the 'free spirit of critical enquiry' but, much more important, for neglecting the Church's solemn responsibility of critical Dogmatics?[1] We are not suggesting that these are more than tendencies in the Church of England, and we know that in these days there are many members of that Church who are acutely aware of them, but at least they are salutary reminders to us that the possession of the 'structure of catholicism' in the traditional sense does not in itself guarantee catholicity according to the apostolic teaching. It is only by

---

[1] And when this is put down to 'the English temperament with its healthy distrust of definition' we are obviously within the sphere of the relative and the sectarian. Perhaps it is only the English who can see nothing incongruous in assuming a vagary of the English temperament to be a mark of catholicity.

looking up to her Lord 'as the eyes of servants look unto the hand of their master'[1] and making herself the instrument of His will that the Church can be sure of her own existence as the Church. Creeds, Liturgy, Ministry, when properly understood, all serve to express the Church's service and to remind her that she lives not from herself but from her Lord, but when their relativity to the living Word is lost sight of and they are made ends in themselves, then they also can become a snare and a delusion. The Church must hear the voice of 'her awin Spouse and Pastor'[2] before she can become the bride of Christ.

The supreme example of this obscuring of the reality of Christ's Lordship in His Church through a misunderstanding of the relation between Christ and His Church is, of course, that which the Roman Church provides. It alone has devoted long and serious attention to the question of the nature of catholicity, and it alone has succeeded in expressing and institutionalizing a denial of catholicity. English Catholicism remains open to the possibility of reformation because the Scriptures remain open in its midst, but Roman Catholicism has succeeded in ruling out the possibility of reformation by its very constitution. The heretical Bishop of Rome is a figure of almost cosmic proportions. Here is none of the pettiness and transitoriness and provincialism of ordinary heresy—though

[1] Psalm cxxiii. 2.
[2] Scots Confession, 1560, Art. XIX.

84

that, no doubt, has its place in the palace intrigues of Italian prelates in the Vatican. The ostentatious grandeur of Saint Peter's, Rome, with its proud flaunting of the 'Tu es Petrus' in letters of gold high above the Table of the Lord, seems to be the perfect historical development of the boasting spirit of him who said, 'Though all men should deny thee, yet will I not deny thee', and the exact opposite of the gracious humility of 'the witness of the suffering of Christ' who had learnt that 'God resisteth the proud, but giveth grace to the humble'.[1] We cannot altogether avoid feeling that in the architecture of Saint Peter's a catholicity of paganism has been achieved. It is at least intelligible how Luther thought of the Pope as antichrist, usurping the throne of Christ. Whatever we may have to say of Luther, we must remember that few men were able to recognize the Devil more surely than he. This is not, of course, to make the infamous suggestion that the architecture of Saint Peter's expresses the whole spirit of the Roman Church or to deny that there are many devout believing Christians in communion with the See of Rome and that the Church of Rome does reveal many of the marks of the true Body of Christ, although grievously disfigured. But the more self-conscious Roman Christianity becomes, the more it carries the tendencies inherent in its constitution to their logical conclusion, as it has a genius for doing, the more openly does it deny the

[1] I Peter v. 5.

necessity of standing *under* the Word of God, and the more boldly does it assert that the voice of the See of Rome *is* the Word of God. Strictly, the Roman doctrine is that the voice of the Pope is the voice of Christ *simpliciter* and that there can be no appeal from the Pope to Christ only when the Pope is defining the nature of the apostolic testimony, the *depositum fidei* itself. But in point of fact the voice of the Pope is listened to un-critically by the faithful on practically every matter on which he wishes to speak, and the attempt is rarely made to examine his utterances in the light of the Word of God.[1] And in view of this, it cannot be without significance that the Roman Church positively encourages a certain unseemly pomp and

[1] In this connection we must confess our bewilderment at the attitude which many younger Anglo-Catholics with whom we have much sympathy take up in regard to Papal pronouncements on modern social and political questions. They are severely critical of their own bishops and very cynical of the possibility of any creative leadership arising from among the 'older theologians' even when they belong to the Anglo-Catholic party. And it seems to us that modern Papal Encyclicals with their dreary platitudes and their complacent self-congratulation are the perfect ex-pression of the spirit they so much distrust in their own leaders. Yet we find them speaking of the 'prophetic lead' which the Pope has given modern Europe! At the risk of appearing invidious, we cannot resist inquiring whether it is not necessary to regard a refusal to be overawed by the much-exploited 'glamour' of the See of Rome as an essential sign of Christian maturity and hence a quality of catholicity.

love of worldy show and power for its own sake. Surely something must be wrong when a Church which is at such pains to emphasize its descent from Saint Peter is content to act and to justify itself in acting in such flagrant contradiction to the instruction Saint Peter himself gives to the elders of the Church.[1] The Reformed Churchman—and this, we admit in penitence, is as much a rebuke to the vulgarized temples of neo-Protestantism with their self-glorification at May Meetings and their 'Rally Sundays' as it is to the Roman Church —will always cry with the Apostle, 'But far be it from me to glory, save in the cross of our Lord Jesus Christ, through which the world hath been crucified unto me, and I unto the world',[2] and be as ready to acknowledge of his Church as of himself that all her righteousnesses are as filthy rags before the Lord.[3]

Rome, then, fails to attain catholicity because she misapprehends the relation in which the Church stands to her Lord. But the Church of Pietism which, for the most part, has been the Church of Protestantism, in England especially, since the eighteenth century, has also failed and. for a similar reason, though in a different way and perhaps not to so great a degree. Certainly no-one dare deny that Pietism know its Lord with a deep and passionate intimacy. It asserts as its most fervent conviction, *ubi Christus, ibi ecclesia*. But emotional intensity and earnestness without the self-

[1] I Peter v.   [2] Gal. vi. 14.   [3] Cf. Isa. vi. 5.

critical activity implied in reformation according to the objective Word of God as He is known in the Scriptures are not enough. By concentrating on 'experience' rather than faith or by having too subjective and emotional a conception of what faith is they missed the fullness of the Gospel.[1] Inevitably they became preoccupied with themselves, and it was their own feelings and prejudices which more and more became the principle of critical judgement in their religious life. That meant that the Christ of the apostolic testimony, Very God 'through whom the worlds were formed' as well

[1] Brunner has explained the process admirably. 'Over against the catchword [of traditional orthodoxy] *fides quae creditur* (the faith that is believed) was set another, *fides qua creditum* (the faith whereby we believe). Once faith has been divided into two parts, into a content true in itself and the "appropriation" of this content, it was inevitable that a movement towards subjectivism should follow by way of reaction against this false objectivism. Reflection was now occupied with religious *experience*, with the processes operated [!] by Scripture, the struggle of repentance, the process of conversion, the inward experience of love to Christ. But when once the main interest is fastened on subjective experience, the objective element, i.e. the Word, dwindles to a mere means of stimulus—for what matters is the "inward working".' (*Philosophy of Religion*, Nicholson & Watson, p. 41.) Cf. *The Basis of Christian Unity, A Statement of the Quaker position prepared for the Second World Conference on Faith and Order to be held at Edinburgh*, 1937. And cf. the way in which Newman misunderstands the Reformed doctrine of faith in terms of this Pietist perversion of it in his *Lectures on Justification*.

as Very Man, became increasingly unintelligible to them, and whole tracts of human life were left outside the sphere of their religious apprehension. Jesus was the sweet Presence Whose love sanctified their inner life and their personal dealings with their neighbours, but they were not conscious that He also claimed the presuppositions of their thoughts and of the society in which they lived for His dominion. The result was that the keener and more sensitive spirits among those brought up in the Churches of Pietism assumed that the Jesus Christ of the apostolic testimony was not Lord in the sense of being the ultimate ground of all reality, and the more positive side of the 'Liberal Modernist' movement can, perhaps, be best understood as the attempt to find another source of ultimate reality which would allow them to find a place for Jesus as the Lord of their personal life. It cannot be too strongly emphasized that in England 'Liberal Modernism' has arisen, for the most part, against the background of Pietism, and can be largely accounted for by the defective catholicity of the Churches of Pietism.[1] English

[1] This accounts for the familiar phenomenon of those 'Liberal Modernist' preachers and theologians who are saved from the unbelief which would be the logical conclusion of their intellectual presuppositions by their vivid sense of the personal presence of Jesus as their Lord. It is well known that this was true in the case of Schleiermacher, who owed much to Moravian influence. Cf. H. R. Mackintosh, *Types of Modern Theology* (Nisbet), p. 86.

Protestantism cannot hope to achieve true reformation unless it sees that.

This fundamental disbelief in the universal Lordship of Jesus Christ which is the root of 'Liberal Modernism' is not expressed in England by elaborate attempts to create a new Dogmatic, after the manner of Schleiermacher's magnificent achievement, but chiefly by an attempt to disprove the Lordship of Jesus through a critical examination of the evidence of the New Testament. Their purpose was, in fact, as we suggested earlier, to confute the testimony of the Apostles, who, from the beginning, had been misled in their understanding of the significance of Jesus. Using the methods of literary and historical criticism they would rediscover Jesus as He was, and men would see His portrait again in all its original fullness undimmed by the 'traditions of men'. In attempting to do this the critics sharpened admirably the weapons of critical scholarship, and for that we are grateful, especially as we are now able to use them against the critics themselves. They were faced with a task of impossible difficulty because the only documents available to them were those left by the Apostles themselves to prove the truth of their testimony concerning Jesus and to guard against precisely the kind of perversions of the Gospel the 'Liberal Modernists' were trying to proclaim. The Gospels were written 'from faith to faith'. They are Church documents and can only be understood within the context of the life of the

Spirit-guided Church. It is only the accidentals of the sacred records which will respond to the methods of ordinary secular historical research. The attempt to ascertain the truth of the Gospel by those methods reveals only that the Gospel's claim to be the ultimate reality which, of necessity, must be self-authenticating and must create the categories necessary for its understanding, has been implicitly denied. The critic must first stand under the κρίσις of the Word of God before he can become truly self-critical and therefore aware of the hindrances he sets in the way of letting the Scriptures speak their message for themselves. Otherwise the unexamined prejudices of his own particular mental and spiritual environment inevitably predispose the critic to find in the Scriptures what he wishes to find, since the method of historical research is in itself inadequate, and he misses the point of the Scriptures. This is what has happened to the 'Liberal Modernists', and it has clearly reflected itself in their characteristic Church forms. Few things belong more completely to their own particular period in history and their own social class and their own educational background than the Unitarian and 'advanced' Congregational Churches of England, all now decaying with the society which produced them. They speak much of the spirit of Jesus as the principle of the Church's catholicity,[1] but what they actually mean

[1] E.g.: 'The Possibility of a United Christendom from the Standpoint of the Congregational Communion', by

by the spirit of Jesus is the idealized expression of their own distinctive ethos to which the Scriptures are conveniently adjusted.[1] We doubt very much whether an Ethiopian or a Russian Christian would recognize in their assemblies the presence of the Christ he knew. We are quite certain that their own children, finding anew through the storms of the twentieth century the rock of the apostolic faith, are bound to confess with heavy hearts that they do not.

The conclusion of our discussion, then, is that the Church finds her catholicity only in making manifest the free Lordship of Jesus Christ. The

C. J. Cadoux in *The Union of Christendom* (S.P.C.K.). This is, perhaps, the best exposition of the nature of catholicity from the English 'Liberal Modernist' point of view, but to claim that this doctrine is that 'which underlies all Congregational classics, and represents the Congregational contribution to the problem of Reunion' (p. 504) is preposterous.

[1] A similar defective catholicity, though admittedly to nothing like the same degree, can be traced in a work of the 'Liberal Catholic' school such as 'Essays Catholic and Critical'—a title which gives the book considerable interest from the point of view of our enquiry. Just because its conception of criticism is derived from the rationalism of post-Renaissance Europe rather than from the $\kappa\rho\iota\sigma\iota\varsigma$ of the Word of God it frequently succeeds in being neither catholic nor critical in the sense which leads inevitably to reformation according to the Word of God, but in being merely 'Anglican' and 'Oxford and Cambridge'. The essay of Sir Edwyn Hoskyns is, of course, a striking exception.

Church cannot attain to the fullness of its life without its Divinely established Order and, as the failure of Pietism warns us, that Order is an important witness to the essence of its life, Jesus Christ, also. But Church Order is not, in itself, the direct expression of the Gospel of God, as the failure of Roman Catholicism warns us. It is through her proclamation, which, as we shall try to show in the next chapter, implies her Order, that the Church makes manifest Christ's free Lordship, through her 'demonstration of the Spirit and of power', so that her own faith and the faith of those who hear may stand not in 'the wisdom of men' but 'in the power of God'. And because that is so, the Church exists always 'in weakness, in fear and in much trembling'. She is always making her act of *confession*, which is completely misunderstood if it is thought of as a bold announcement of her unchallengeable catholicity or, from the other side, as mere scholastic logic-chopping. It is the confession of the Church's repentance, her recognition that she is always in danger of falling away from the Truth by which she lives and her acknowledgement that in her proclamation she is concerned above all things to give the glory, not to herself, but to her Lord. Therefore, the truly Catholic Church, knowing that at best she is but an 'earthen vessel', pleads always with each of her members that if he find in her proclamation anything 'repugnant to God's holie Word, that it wold pleis him of his gentleness

93

and for Christian charities sake to admonish us of the same in writing; and we upon our honoures and fidelitie, be God's grace do promise unto him satisfaction fra the mouth of God, that is fra his holy Scriptures, or else reformation of that quhilk he sal prove to be amisse',[1] that in all things 'the exceeding greatness of the power may be of God, and not from ourselves'.

[1] Preface to the Scots Confession of 1560.

Chapter IV

THE ORDINANCE OF GOD:
THE CATHOLIC CHURCH AND THE
CATHOLIC CHRISTIAN

We turn now to examine in greater detail what Reformed theology calls the Ordinance of God for His Church, which is, it is useful to realize, very much what Ramsey means by 'the structure of catholicism'. Here we shall be dealing with what we may call the secondary marks of catholicity, those which express the fullness of the Church as well as its essence. The distinction between essence and fullness must not be pressed because, of course, the form of the Church arises out of the Gospel and is designed to witness to the Gospel, but it is valuable both for convenience of exposition and because it reminds us that, as we have seen, the 'structure of catholicism' depends for its catholicity upon the Gospel and is not itself the Gospel.

The Catholic Christian is the man who stands under the judgement and promise of God through Jesus Christ in the Holy Ghost. He arrives at his true membership of the Church, his catholic status, through Baptism by which he is incorporated into Christ. The Sacrament of Baptism, in a pre-eminent way, brings home to us that the essence of the Church is the presence of Jesus Christ. But, because the Church exists in a fallen world, the possibility of falling away from his Baptism is always before the Christian, as well as the necessity of expressing its reality in terms of his life on this earth. He needs, therefore, constantly to be re-assured of his membership of Jesus Christ and to mark off his own life, in community with his fellow members, from the form of this world which passeth away. This happens in the Church's Divine Service. The Christian 'examines himself', according to the exhortation of the Apostle, scrutinizing his whole existence in the light of God's Word, Jesus Christ, and is thus moved to repentance and faith, crying 'My Lord and My God'. This is typified by the preaching of the Word in Divine Service in the narrower sense on the Lord's Day. Then he embraces Jesus Christ, the veritable Jesus Christ, His body and His blood, and in so doing finds his own true manhood, by the restoration of God's image in him through his incorporation into Jesus Christ. This is typified by the Sacrament of the Lord's Supper, which completes and fulfils the preaching of the Word. Thus the first of the secondary marks of the Church's catholicity is the possession of this liturgical form and with it the clear recognition that the rhythm of repentance, faith, newness of life, expressed in Divine Service on the Lord's Day, is that of the Church's own life, without which she dies. Once again, it is a striking indication of the failure of the so-called Reformed Churches to understand their true nature that they have frequently not grasped this indispensable relation between Divine Service and the Church's continued existence as the true Church and, therefore, of the individual believer's continued existence as a Catholic Christian. The proof of this is the fact that for the most part the Reformed Churches have, until very recently, neglected to insist upon the inner coherence of preaching and Sacrament every Lord's Day.[1] Even at the dawn of the Reformation itself it is doubtful whether this relation was clearly seen, as it is well known that Calvin himself was not able to establish the dispensing of the Sacrament every Lord's Day in Geneva. Later, of course, when preaching came to be understood as 'edifying discourse' or 'truth through personality' the confusion became much worse. The true preaching of the Word and faithful administration of the Sacraments which are the marks of the presence of Christ in the Church do not mean merely 'Biblical' preaching in the formal, conventional sense, and occasional Sacramental services performed according to a seemly traditional order. They mean much more that the

[1] Cf. the important criticism of modern Protestant services in Barth, *The Knowledge of God and the Service of God*, pp. 211–12.

Church should recognize the mutual relations of preaching and Sacraments and of the Sacraments with each other and that, in turn, she should understand their relation to her own existence as the Church. Therefore, whatever takes place in the Church's service 'must have its origin in Baptism, in the *existence* of the Church, in the three-fold fact that Jesus Christ has once and for all died and risen again for us, that we are irrevocably His and that we are destined for no other end than to be justified, sanctified, and glorified through Him. And whatever takes place in the Church service must have as its end the *Lord's Supper*, the *continuance* of the Church, Jesus Christ's giving us a new share in His existence as man as existence with God and the constant fulfilment of our destiny, which is to be the object of His work.'[1] Thus the Church's Divine Service, her λειτουργία, is her chief means of making manifest Christ's Lordship in her own midst and, understood in this sense, we can agree entirely with traditional Catholicism that the possession of the Liturgy is an essential mark of catholicity. From this point of view, perhaps we may say cautiously that the Liturgical Movement among Roman Catholics does remind us that we must not necessarily give up hope of being able to reach an understanding with each other on this matter. Both traditional Catholicism and traditional Protestantism have

[1] Barth, *The Knowledge of God and the Service of God*, p. 195.

lost the true meaning of the Liturgy and we need each other's witness in rediscovering it. But we can only hope to do so if we seek to interpret it in terms of Jesus Christ, Very God and Very Man, Who is the heart of the Liturgy.[1]

In order that the Divine service of the Church may be properly performed the service of the apostolic Ministry is essential. The possession of the apostolic Ministry is, thus, the second of the

---

[1] Cf. Hebert, *Liturgy and Society*, p. 132. The theological purpose of the Liturgy is very clearly expressed by such Anglo-Catholic writers as Fathers Hebert and Ramsey, e.g. 'Saint Paul's prayers are not primarily petitions, nor primarily mystical acts of contemplation; they are primarily LITURGICAL, not in the sense that he reads them out of a book but (in the more fundamental sense of the word 'liturgy') that his method is first to recall the action of God, in Christ's redemption and in the one Body, and only then to utter his petitions by bringing into this action the topical needs with which he is concerned' (Ramsey, *The Gospel and the Catholic Church*, p. 89). It is important to have this more fundamental sense of the word 'Liturgy' made clear and to distinguish it from its secondary sense as a set form of service. In John Owen's *Discourse Concerning Liturgies* he really means what Ramsey means by the deeper sense of the word 'Liturgy' when he speaks of 'the institutions and ordinances of Christ in the outward worship of God'. He goes on to contrast this with the 'set forms' which he rejects as 'man-made'. Whether he was right in doing this we shall discuss later, but it is important to see that the seventeenth-century Congregational divine and the modern Anglo-Catholic are agreed in making what Ramsey calls the 'Liturgy' in the more fundamental sense a mark of the Church's catholicity.

secondary marks of the Church's catholicity. Here, at least, traditional Catholicism is in the right as against 'Liberal Modernism', Pietism, and 'lay religion', as Forsyth used to say, of all kinds. Reformed theology does not quarrel with traditional Catholicism because of its insistence that possession of the apostolic Ministry is a mark of catholicity, but because of its identification of that Ministry with the historical monarchical episcopate and its justification of it, not on the properly theological grounds of continuity with the apostolic testimony, but on the relative, mundane grounds of mere historical connection or secular theories of government. The apostolic Ministry is essential to the Church's existence because, as we have seen, it is through its proclamation, which implies its having undergone the κρίσις of the Word of God in the most responsible and comprehensive sense through the discipline of critical Dogmatics, that the Church's service of God becomes a real offering of herself in Jesus Christ and a real offering of Jesus Christ to the world, the Jesus Christ Who is the content of the apostolic testimony and whose veritable coming 'in the flesh' can be known only through the apostolic testimony. And this holds of the Sacraments as well as of preaching, for it is only when the elements are received in faith, only, that is, when men have made that movement away from themselves to find their true humanity in Jesus Christ which is the movement of Divine Service, that they become the body and blood of

Christ and hence the Church His Sacramental body. We are compelled, therefore, to insist in the strongest possible fashion that the Ministry of Word and Sacraments and the Ministry of the Dogmatic theologian which is involved in the Ministry of Word and Sacraments, the 'professional' Ministry in the most deliberate and self-conscious sense, is an indispensable mark of the Church and in no sense, as modern Protestantism has sometimes tended to imagine, a luxury which she can afford to enjoy only where she is well established and most certainly not a 'formalizing' and 'legalizing' corruption which, in the course of history, has come between the simple, natural piety of the ordinary believer and the primitive purity of the teaching of the 'Jesus of history'. Where the apostolic Ministry does not exist the Church has not the form of catholicity.

It is, perhaps, necessary to say that this, of course, does not mean that the Ministry is the heart of the Church's life and that the congregation exists only on its circumference. That is a mistake which, in different ways, both traditional Catholicism and neo-Protestantism have tended to make. The Ministry is only a function in the Church, a means by which all members are enabled to hear the true Word of God and live the true Christian life. It is the servant of the Church's service. It exists in order to deliver the Church from all human arrogance and pretension and is her effort to make sure that Jesus Christ and He alone is acknowledged in her midst as Lord. As Barth says of theology, 'It enquires if our hearing of God's Word is being duly qualified and it enquires about the adequacy of our proclamation and perception in relation to the institution of the church as established by Jesus Christ. It asks the church about her sincerity and humility. To this extent theology, too, belongs to the church service and is itself a leaven for the church's liturgy.'[1]

It is because this responsible theological activity is part of the Ministry's function in the Church, without which the Church's proclamation is impossible, that we are not disposed to give the Oecumenical Creeds the status of marks of catholicity. We in no way deny their relative authority and recognize their unique place in the life of the Church, both because of their ultimate apostolic origin and because of their expressing the Church's inevitable exegesis of the heart of the apostolic testimony in terms of the doctrine of the Trinity and of the Two Natures. But, in the end, the authority they possess does not differ in kind from that which the Church's *confession* always possesses. They are subject to and controlled by the Scriptures and they are the fruits of the Church's critical endeavour to listen to the voice of the Scriptures. Given the Scriptures and the apostolic Ministry, the Church will reach the same conclusions as do the Creeds. Given the Creeds without a true understanding of the Scriptures on the part

[1] *The Knowledge of God and the Service of God*, p. 216.

of the Ministry, the Church will not necessarily hear the voice of Jesus Christ, the Word of God. The Creeds, then, are an invaluable witness to the true meaning of the Scriptures, and no Church which rejected them could be called catholic, but since they depend for their true understanding on factors other than themselves, acceptance of the Creeds by itself cannot be deemed a mark of the Church's catholicity.

When we say that possession of the apostolic Ministry in the sense we have defined is an indispensable mark of the Church's catholicity we mean that it is a mark of the fullness of the Church and that where it does not exist the Church's essence is imperilled. We are not going so far as to say that bodies which do not possess it are not Christian and, therefore, in some way a part of the Church. For these bodies,[1] such as the Society of Friends or those modern Congregational Churches whose

---

[1] We cannot shut out the possibility, of course, that God may call all the members of a Church to the office of ministry, so that a 'professional' ministry in the narrower sense may not be needed. It is on the assumption that this has, in fact, happened that such bodies as the Plymouth Brethren work. While there is a sense in which it is true that, as we shall go on to seek to show, the Church as a whole is the custodian of the apostolic testimony, we are bound, however, to inquire whether Scripture and experience do not prove that the Ministry is a particular office in the Church to which particular members are ordained of God. Cf. John Owen, *The Duty of Pastors and People Distinguished*, in vol. xix of his Works (London, 1826).

ministers, with the consent of their congregations, are not concerned to conform their testimony to that of the Apostles, all live—in so far as they are alive as Churches at all—secondarily and derivatively by the Word of God. The Word of God has entry into their assemblies, and even though it may fall on stony ground it is not for us to deny that it may bear fruit. But the point is that the forms of their Churches are not designed to witness to and proclaim God's Lordship in Jesus Christ. They do not possess the outward marks of catholicity. They are not equipped to be 'Independent' Churches.

The concept of the 'Independent' Church needs to be entirely re-examined and re-stated. When it is done, we are sure that apparently irreconcilable points of view will be seen to be much nearer each other than we had ever realized. It has been a disaster that in our English situation the Independents developed their doctrine of the Church against the background of the peculiar Anglican conception of the 'National' Church. The consequence has been that attention has been concentrated on the idea of the 'gathered' as opposed to the 'territorial' Church, and the fullness of the New Testament doctrine of the Church has been lost in partisan controversy. The idea of the 'Independent' Church is simply an attempt to take seriously the catholicity of the visible Church. To call a Church an 'Independent' Church is to say that it is a 'Catholic' Church—a Church, that is, which bears all the marks of the Church's catholicity upon itself and does not need, therefore, to derive any spiritual sustenance or authority from outside its own life. An 'Independent' Church is one which possesses all the ordinances appointed by its Lord for ministering Him to the world and which is therefore able to stand on its own spiritual feet and to act responsibly as the Church of God in the place where it is set. Where a Church possesses Scriptures, Proclamation, the Sacraments, the Apostolic Ministry and, as we shall go on to show, the Church Meeting, it is equipped —under God—for God's service, for manifesting Jesus Christ to the world and walking in His way, and no body can be more truly or more fully the Church than it. For it is these which are the marks of catholicity and it is through them alone that catholicity can be mediated. Modern Independency has almost entirely lost sight of this fact and, as a consequence, has frequently been a denial of true 'Independency'. It has misunderstood the text, 'Where two or three are gathered together in my name, there am I in the midst of them' to mean that any group of people who announced that they were gathered together in Christ's name were the Church of Christ and possessed the fullness and the freedom of the Church of Christ, and has overlooked the fact that it is only the presence of the Word, Sacraments, and Apostolic Ministry with Dogmatics which can ensure that the gathering

together is in fact in Christ's name.[1] Because of
this we have not realized that the Church Order
of traditional Catholicism is, in fact, that of 'Independency', though corrupted in its Roman form
by the Papacy and in its Anglican form by secular
ideas of administration. A diocese is a large-scale
model of an 'Independent' Church, just as a
modern properly organized Congregational Church
is a small-scale model. If the Lambeth Quadrilateral were to substitute the words 'Apostolic
Ministry' for the words 'historic episcopate' there
would be no ultimate ground for division between
true 'Independency' and the Church of England.
The structure of the Church has become overlaid
with such a mass of extraneous material in England
in recent centuries that both the Church of England and the 'Independent' Churches have almost
entirely lost all understanding of the essential form
of their own churches, and unless we try to understand again what the real 'structure of catholicism' is
we shall never be able to achieve real re-union. We
shall succeed only in readjusting the relationships
of vaguely ecclesiastical organizations to each other.

[1] Cf. Nathaniel Micklem, *Congregationalism To-day*
(Hodder & Stoughton, 1937), p. 7. It is significant that
the context of the famous phrase *ubi Christus, ibi ecclesia* is
the following: 'Let that be a valid Eucharist which is
celebrated in the presence of a Bishop or one appointed by
him. Where the Bishop is there also let the people be, even
as where Christ Jesus is, there is the universal church (*ubi
Christus, ibi ecclesia*).' Saint Ignatius, *Ad Smyrn.*, viii,
quoted in Congar, *Divided Christendom*, p. 88.

It is along the lines of this new understanding of the nature of 'Independency' that we can also discern the possibility of a new understanding of the nature of the episcopal office. The whole trend of our argument demands that Churches do not exist in isolation from each other or, indeed, that there can be any other than the one Church. The conditions of human existence are such that we must all hold our membership in a particular congregation of Christ's people. Our membership would be unreal, it would be a denial of the Church's historicity and stubborn particularity if that were not so. But that membership is in the true and complete Church as it exists in the place where we are set. As Ramsey puts it, '. . . the ἐκκλησία in a place is the *one race* as existing in that place, e.g., the "ecclesia" of Corinth is the one called-out race of God which exists in Corinth, as in many other places'.[1] And as John Owen put it: 'I say then that the true and only union of all particular churches consists in that which gives form, life and being unto the church catholic, with the addition of what belongs unto them as they are in particular. And this is, that they have all one and the same God and Father, one Lord Jesus Christ, one faith and one doctrine of faith, one hope of their calling on the promised inheritance, one regeneration, one baptism, one bread and wine, united unto God and Christ in one Spirit,

[1] *The Gospel and the Catholic Church*, p. 47.

through the bond of faith and love.'[1] Further, as it is again John Owen who says, it is imperative that particular Churches should hold communion with each other, since 'the end of their institution and being' is 'the glory of Christ in the edification of the whole catholic church'.[2] This communion of particular Churches is, from the point of view of order, to be expressed, according to John Owen, through synods and councils. We are not here attempting to give an exhaustive account of Church Order and, especially in view of our confusion on these questions, it would be unwise to state all the functions of such synods at this point—although we would mention the preparation of the Church's Confession of Faith and the disciplining of Churches which had fallen away from the Faith as among the chief—but we must insist that they are to be regarded as essential to the fullness of the Church's life. And in view of the special place of the Ministry in the Church's life as in a very direct way the successor to the Apostles who testified of Jesus Christ, it is fitting that the particular Church should be represented at such synods by its minister. As the one who declares the Gospel in the Church, it is he who can most clearly represent the Church's unity in Jesus Christ to other

[1] John Owen, D.D., 'Of the Communion of the Churches', ch. xi of *The True Nature of a Gospel Church and its Government*, Works, vol. xx (London, 1826), p. 576.

[2] *The True Nature of a Gospel Church and its Government*, p. 579.

Churches. Certainly we cannot agree that a synod of ministers is any more the Catholic Church than the Church Meeting of a particular Church. It is the one Church, living by the same Spirit, responsible to the same Lord, in both cases. The difference between the two is one of function only. But the synod of ministers has the authority which inheres in its function in the same way as the Church Meeting has. The point about which we are not clear at present is whether there is any fundamental difference between this doctrine and the doctrine of episcopacy expounded by Father Hebert in his admirable pamphlet, *Unity and the Truth*.[1] The confusion in the past has been due to the fact that episcopacy has been thought of nearly always in terms of the monarchical episcopate and that the Independent doctrine of the Ministry has nearly always been developed in polemical opposition to it. If it were recognized on the one hand that the episcopate as we know it, especially in England, has been corrupted by secular ideas of administration so that it is the presbyter rather than the bishop who to-day performs most of the functions of the bishop in apostolic times,[2] and on the other hand that the local congregation is the Church Catholic in a particular place and cannot fulfil its true nature without holding communion with other Churches and that the office of the Ministry

[1] Pages 45–52 (S.P.C.K., 1939). Cf. Ramsey, pp. 81–5, and *Liturgy and Society*, ch. iii.

[2] Cf. *Unity in the Truth*, p. 49.

is the organ of the Church's unity, then we are sure that discussion would proceed on a much more hopeful basis.[1]

The possession of the apostolic Ministry in the local church and, as representing the local church, in synods, is then a secondary mark of catholicity. But if that is so, we must hasten to add that possession of what Congregationalists call the Church Meeting is also a secondary mark of catholicity. The exact constitution of the Church Meeting is an open question, but the truth to which the Congregational conception of the Church Meeting witnesses—and it is, perhaps, the greatest contribution of the Congregational Churches to the fullness of the Church's catholicity—is that there must be an organ in the Church's life through which all who have attained to the fullness of the stature of manhood in Jesus Christ shall be able to express their responsibility before God for living the full Christian life and for obeying His ordinance in the Church. The Church Meeting, according to the true genius of Congregationalism, is not merely a means for cultivating the spiritual life like a Methodist Class Meeting, nor is it an

[1] In this connection we recommend strongly to both Anglicans and modern Congregationalists the chapter in Owen which we have already quoted. Allowing for the fact that he assumes, with after all some justice, that the episcopate is necessarily the secularized monarchical episcopate, it remains the most authoritative statement on catholicity from the Reformed point of view in our English situation.

application of the methods of secular democracy to the government of the Church.[1] Within its sphere, and we agree that the limits of that sphere should be much more carefully defined than has yet been done, it is as serious and responsible an organ of the life of the Catholic Church as is a synod of bishops within its sphere. Congregationalists should not regard it as their special theory of Church government, which fits in well with the modern democratic spirit, in the same way as Broad Churchmen in the Church of England defend the monarchical episcopate on the ground of its 'proved efficiency'. They should regard it as an attempt at a fuller articulation of 'the structure of catholicism' than any other body has yet achieved, which presupposes for its effective working the overruling authority of the Scriptures, the Liturgy in the sense we have defined, and the apostolic Ministry possessing the authority necessary for the fulfilment of its proper function. Where these do not exist the Church Meeting, as modern Congregational Churches have good cause to know, reveals all the faults of irresponsible mass democracy at its worst. Where they do exist, it fills up what is the most obvious and weakening gap in the life of traditional Catholicism.

[1] Though we do not deny that even in the seventeenth century the Rationalism of the Renaissance influenced its development along the lines it actually took. *Vide* Perry Miller, *The New England Mind* (MacMillan, New York, 1939), ch. xiii.

The trouble with traditional Catholicism in practice—and this is true of Presbyterianism also to some extent—is that the ordinary member has little opportunity of expressing his membership of the Church except through his attendance at Divine Service and his obedience to his pastors.[1] Indeed, he is not so much a member of the Church, through whom the life-blood of the Church flows, as a person who derives his spiritual sustenance from the Church, which appears to exist in some way independently of him. He is the Church's child who is not allowed to take upon himself the responsibilities of spiritual manhood, but lives perpetually in the period between Baptism and Confirmation. The lack of inwardness in the traditional Catholic understanding of the Sacraments is re-

[1] 'The Church is the mystical Body of Christ, a Body ruled by Pastors and Teachers, a society of men headed by rulers having full and perfect powers of governing, instructing and judging. It follows that this Church is essentially an unequal society, that is to say, a society comprising two categories of persons; pastors and the flock; those who hold rank in the different degrees of the hierarchy and the multitude of the faithful; and these categories are so distinct in themselves that in the pastoral body alone reside the necessary right and authority to guide and direct all the members towards the goal of the society. As for the multitude, it has no other right than that of allowing itself to be led and, as a docile flock, to follow its shepherds.' From the Encyclical of Pope Pius X, *Vehementer*, 11 February 1906, quoted in J. S. Whale, *Christian Doctrine* (Cambridge University Press, 1941), pp. 133–4.

vealed by the fact that the members' participation in them appears to bear no relation to their function in the Body. In a properly ordered Congregational Church admission to the Sacrament of the Lord's Supper carries with it admission to the responsibilities of membership of the Church Meeting. By partaking of the Sacrament, the Christian declares that he is no longer 'in ward', but has attained to spiritual maturity. He has laid hold on his true manhood by embracing Jesus Christ in faith under the veils of the bread and wine, and in so doing has found true community with his fellows. He is ready for living, then, as a responsible person in the family of Christ's people, and the Church Meeting, gathered together at the hearth of the household of faith after the family have been fed at the Lord's Table, is the means through which he can do so. He has the right to share in all the joys and sorrows, the privileges and the burdens, of the household and to speak his mind in his turn as the Spirit gives him utterance with the freedom of the Christian man. This does not mean that the Church is at the mercy of 'lay religion' precisely because the Church Meeting exists within the context of the whole life of the Church. The member, when he raises his voice in Church Meeting, speaks under the authority of the Word of God and in the unity of the Spirit as he knows it in the Sacrament and with due heed to the counsel of the Apostolic Ministry. Indeed, unless he does speak in this responsible manner he cannot be sure that he is speaking as a Christian. It is a striking testimony to the spiritual vitality of traditional Catholicism that it produces so many vigorous 'laymen's' movements, but an astonishing commentary on the inadequacy of its Church Order that it can find no place for them in 'the structure of catholicism'. The result is that such movements are always in danger of theological irresponsibility and therefore of heresy, since their members cannot bring their actions under the scrutiny of the Word of God in the fellowship of His family. And this danger cannot be satisfactorily averted by the artificial method of external clerical control, for the obedience of the member of the Church must be a free, personal obedience to Jesus Christ, the Head, and not merely conformity to regulations laid down by a clergy.

It is true that sectarian neo-Protestantism has not clearly understood the function of the Ministry in the Church but, on the other hand, it is difficult to see how traditional Catholicism is able to distinguish between the Ministry and the Church. The congregation, indeed, seems to be something of an embarrassment in traditional Catholicism. This is seen in the way in which religious devotion is canalized into Orders. As soon as an ordinary member shows a desire to take his Christian profession seriously the only thing to do is to recommend him to join an Order, since as a member of the congregation he has nothing to do except to be faithful and obedient to his ministers. The truth is, however, that as modern Catholicism realizes as clearly as modern Protestantism the responsibility for the well-being of the Church rests on every member, though members may have different gifts and functions, and that every member must be given freedom to follow Christ according to his calling. Father Hebert, in a striking chapter on 'The Church Service'[1] says that 'Christian worship is in the first place a confession of faith in God and a commemoration of God's work of salvation; and then an expression of the application of that salvation to the whole of human life.' We agree and we agree heartily with his description of the purpose of the Parish Eucharist, but we are bound to inquire whether, if the worship is 'an expression of the application of that salvation to the whole of human life' it does not need something rather more responsible and workmanlike than a Parish Breakfast to follow it, whether, in fact, the unity of the Body which has been realized in the Communion does not need something like what Congregationalists call the Church Meeting.

The real trouble appears to be that traditional Catholicism will not admit that the Ministry is merely a function in the Church, but is determined to regard the Ministry alone as living the full Christian life and the congregation as doing so only derivatively from it. It will not, ultimately, allow itself to agree with Barth when he says,

[1] *Liturgy and Society*, ch. ix. Cf. Barth, *Knowledge of God and Service of God*, pp. 212–13.

'Holy Scripture itself governs the church. The ecclesiastical order *and* the congregation are not lords over it but organs serving it',[1] for he goes on to say, 'The ecclesiastical order has its life solely in the congregation, but the congregation has not its life solely in the ecclesiastical order. The freedom of the Word of God and the legitimate authority of the decisions and obligations necessary in the church are less menaced when the constitution makes it clear that it is not some few members of the church but all of them who are called and qualified to be vigilant and faithful and, what is more, to be so with equal seriousness, and where the holders of special offices have to speak and act only as *primi inter pares*, joint responsibility being shared by all the rest.' The Reformed churchman will agree that the minister has to lead, in one sense, a life of 'vicarious catholicity' on behalf of the congregation, being set apart by them for living more directly under the Word of God than the majority of them, busy with buying and selling and marrying and being given in marriage, are able to, in order that he may be an 'example to the flock', both by way of warning and of inspiration. He has to be the self-consciousness of the Church, where the Church 'examines itself' in the light of the Word of God, and thus he makes manifest both the tribulation of the Church[2] and the glory of the Church in his own person. He must so know the Word of God and the human nature it addresses

[1] *Knowledge of God and Service of God*, p. 185.
[2] 1 Cor. iv. 9–13.   116

as to be both prophet and priest to the people in Jesus Christ. And, as Barth says, 'In the service the speaking as such is the concern of some and not of others, and this is a parable which may not be set aside—a parable of the fact that God speaks but it is man's task to listen.'[1] There is a way, therefore, in which the Ministry is representative of the whole life of the Church. Yet it is this only for the sake of the Church and within the fellowship of the Church. It is still only a function of the Body and not the Body itself. However formally perfect the work of the Ministry in a Church may be, unless that work is expressed and fulfilled in the life of the congregation by the creation and sustenance of men who find their true humanity as responsible persons serving God in His Church, then that Church has not the form of catholicity. There is a danger, even, in thinking of the task of the Ministry as primarily the cure of souls and not that of proclamation. The minister is not responsible for the souls of his people to God. Every man must answer for himself to God and he can speak only the one word—Jesus Christ. The minister is but the chief of the 'helps' in the Church, who is able to assist his people 'who are slow of speech and of a slow tongue' when they take that word upon their lips. In this connection we cannot ponder too much the story of the appointment of Aaron in Exodus iv. 10–16. The minister is not himself the Good Shepherd. He is

[1] *Knowledge of God and Service of God*, p. 213.

merely the Shepherd's boy who keeps an eye on the flock in accordance with his Master's instruction and who leads them to where they can find green pastures.[1] The Church knoweth her 'awin Spouse and Pastor' and He alone is the Bishop of our souls. Certainly the minister must express the pastoral concern of Christ, which is love of the brethren, towards his people, but that is what all the brethren, who are rooted and grounded in that same love, should do for each other, building up each other in the faith. Similarly, the minister must, as traditional Catholicism insists, witness to and represent Christ in all his actions, in teaching and visiting as well as in preaching and dispensing the Sacraments, but surely the fullness of catholic truth is that we must all witness to and represent Christ to each other, according to our several vocations, so that it is no longer we who live but Christ in us. The question of the mutual relations and authority of minister and people comes more directly under the heading of the doctrine of the Church proper. For our present purpose it is sufficient to note that the presence in the Church of an organ which gives expression to the personal existence in responsibility of every member of Christ's body is an essential mark of catholicity.[2]

[1] John xxi. 15–17.
[2] It seems to us that this is recognized by Father Hebert in a very important passage in *Liturgy and Society*, pp. 230–4, where he distinguishes between the Liberal-democratic theory of government, that the best form is

The distinctive mark of the Catholic Christian is, indeed, this responsible personal existence which is the fullness of the stature of true manhood. It is Luther's 'freedom of the Christian man' who is no longer under law but under grace. Any accusation against traditional Catholicism must carry with it a humble acknowledgement of the failures of neo-Protestantism also in this matter, but we are bound to inquire whether in practice the Churches of traditional Catholicism are much more than a παιδαγωγός to bring men to Christ, keeping them in ward until they attain to spiritual maturity through justification by faith, rather than the community of the sons of God in Jesus Christ.[1] Indeed, as far as we can gather, traditional Catholicism conceives of the Church alone as attaining to the fullness of manhood and of the individual members as merely sharing, in varying degrees, in

'that of an assembly in which various interests meet in conflict and the vote of the majority prevails', and government in the Church which is a Body and which, therefore, must try to seek a common mind among its members, an attempt which is possible 'because the Church's existence is based on a common faith'. The method of government adopted at Kelham differs little from the proper form of government in a Congregational Church, although the people have safeguards against an irresponsible decision of the Ministry, and in spite of all the errors of modern Congregationalism its meaning has never been entirely lost. Cf. P. T. Forsyth, *The Principle of Authority*, and cf. T. M. Lindsay, *The Church and Ministry in the Early Centuries* (Hodder & Stoughton, 1902), pp. 58–9.

[1] Gal. iii. 23–6.

that manhood. It is true that so deeply evangelical a Roman Catholic as Father Congar is able to describe the truly Catholic Christian as one who 'knows himself to be by grace the son of the Father, and radiates the likeness of God in sufficient measure as to be recognized as a member incorporate with those who are also of the family of God and bear the stamp of Christ's likeness',[1] and that such books as Maritain's *True Humanism* reveal a rich understanding of Christian personal existence, but we are puzzled to know how far their attitude is compatible with other strains in Roman Catholic teaching. It is, no doubt, unfair to say out of hand that Catholicism, both Roman and Anglican, depersonalizes the relation between Christ and the believer and has a merely quantitative conception of grace, but even the most inward of Catholic theologians do not altogether escape this danger, while it undoubtedly happens almost universally in Catholic Church life. Certainly there are treatises without number on the cultivation of the spiritual life, but the emphasis is on attaining an ever higher degree of individual holiness rather than upon bringing forth the fruits of the Spirit through the full personal integration which is the inevitable concomitant of that identification of Jesus Christ, Very Man, with each one of us, the subjective side of which we call justifying faith. And can it be an accident that while Catholicism develops its doctrine of the Church and of the

[1] *Divided Christendom*, p. 114.

Ministry from supernatural revelation, it is compelled to derive much of its teaching about the 'walk and conversation' of the ordinary member from Natural Law, which, however much it is refined, is not the same thing as that λογική λατρεία which involves, for all the brethren, being fashioned not according to this world but being transformed by the renewing of our minds?

The Churches of the Reformation have little reason for glorying in their history since the seventeenth century, but they can claim, as against traditional Catholicism in the same period, that they have succeeded in creating men who have some marks of the 'Liberty of the Christian Man' about them and who are able to live and act as integrated, responsible persons, 'fearing God always and man never'. It is true that, in the course of history, their descendants were transformed into the disintegrated individualists of secular Liberal democracy, and that this was largely due to the Church's failure to understand the true 'structure of catholicism'[1] which ensures that the Spirit is always the Spirit of the Word and never the free, adventurous human spirit of modern man. But, at the same time, the Protestant 'rediscovery of the individual' was not the assertion of mere sinful egotism, disrupting the organic unity of Christ's body. It was the rediscovery of true humanity, the

[1] But not to Luther's alleged misunderstanding of the nature of Christian liberty, as Congar claims, *Divided Christendom*, p. 122.

reclamation of our true heritage as sons of God and brethren of each other, united in a common relationship to Christ, a common faith, and a common obedience, even though our functions in the life of the Household are different. Once again, Catholics may assert that this does not contradict the inwardness of their own doctrine. That may well be true, but we are compelled in turn to ask whether the whole spirit and practice of traditional Catholicism do not contradict it. There is not merely the undeniable difference in status between the hierarchy and the laity which traditional Catholicism is at every point concerned to emphasize. There is the positive discouragement of the ordinary members of the Church from attaining to the fullness of the stature of manhood. It is the simple faith of the unlettered peasant which is idealized by traditional Catholicism in its most characteristic forms. The congregation are the 'dear children' of the hierarchy. But in point of fact they are nothing of the kind. They are the brethren of their ministers and have a right to protest when it is assumed that they should be fed on milk, as babes in Christ, and that the meat should be reserved for the 'religious'. Faith is the act by which we appropriate our true manhood and declare our spiritual maturity. In the act of faith we have restored to us that capacity for making responsible decisions in freedom which is the mark of true personal existence and which we had lost through sin. Unless a man can give a 'reason for the faith that is in him', not so much in the sense of being able to explain it intellectually as in the sense of being sure of its inner consistency and of its being a key to the meaning of all life then his faith is not a true faith. There is a good deal of nonsense talked about simple faith both by traditional Catholics and romantic Liberals. An element of 'sophistication' is inseparable from genuine Christian faith. The Christian in this world must know the Devil for what he is if he is truly to know Christ and His redeeming work. Certainly he possesses the simplicity and spontaneity of little children because he has now found the true centre of existence in Jesus Christ, but he is not naïve or childish. Like Kierkegaard he has to *realize* the universal human, he has to achieve spontaneity *after* reflection. He has to *become* as a little child. He has not to be so weak and gullible as never to cease being a little child and certainly he is not to be encouraged in those qualities of weakness and gullibility in the name of pastoral concern. The Catholic Christian must be an instructed Christian. He must know that it is by Christ alone that he is saved and that it is in His power and by the illumination of His Spirit that he lives, and he must be able to distinguish the voice of Christ from his own voice and that of the world. He must know the Scriptures so that he can feed his faith at the source and not be dependent for his faith on the word of the preacher, even though he should be obedient to the word of the preacher when he understands, from his own knowledge of the Word of God, that the word of the preacher is the Word of God. And he must know enough about the world in which he is set and his place in it to know how best he can fulfil his vocation in it as a Christian and make responsible decisions for which he will be himself answerable to God. He must be able to bring all his life into the κρίσις of the Word of God, leaving none of the presuppositions of his existence unexamined and testing all the spirits which confront him in the world, to see whether they be of Christ. To say that this is impossible to the ordinary believer is to assert that God is incapable of stirring up in men the gifts necessary for obeying Him, and the experience of the Church proves abundantly that it is possible. There are Welsh miners of our acquaintance who possess more mature Catholic judgement than many elaborately educated ministers. Nothing is a clearer sign of a lack of true catholicity than the attempt to set arbitrary limits to the sphere of God's sovereignty and to the power of God's grace, and it is in this respect, above all others, that the so-called 'Catholic' Churches have failed most completely.

Chapter V

QUALITIES OF THE CATHOLIC CHURCH

In discussing the marks of the Church's catholicity, our attention was concentrated on her form, the means by which she finds her true life in Jesus Christ. In this chapter we shall try to enumerate some of the qualities which the Church should display if she has in fact found her true life in Jesus Christ. This is not an account of the 'fruits of the Spirit' which 'they that are of Christ Jesus' will always bring forth, but an attempt to state some of the ways in which the Church can prove to herself not merely that she possesses but also that she understands the proper significance of 'the structure of catholicism'.

Firstly, then, the Catholic Church must be one Church, even as Jesus Christ her Lord is one. Christ is not divided, therefore His body is not divided. There is 'one Lord, one faith, one baptism, one God and Father of all, Who is over all, and through all, and in all', and therefore all who are His must give diligence 'to keep the unity of the

spirit in the bond of peace'. The magnificent exposition of the oneness of the Church which Father
Congar gives[1] is vitiated for us by his sharing the
Roman Catholic misunderstanding of the nature of
faith which makes it difficult for him to distinguish
between the Church and her Lord,[2] but he is being
true to the Scriptures when he bases the oneness
of the Church on the unity of the Blessed Trinity
and when he says: 'It is because there is only one
God that there is only one Church, one with the
very oneness of God, outside Whom she does not
exist. Because we participate in one life, which is
the life of God, we are one with God and one
among ourselves, in Christ.'[3] And he is right also
when he insists that this oneness must be expressed
in the visible form of the Church on this earth,
even though we cannot accept his account of the
marks of that visible form or its relation to the
Lord Whom it manifests. The unity of the Spirit
has no content, does not genuinely exist in terms
of our life on this earth, if it is not expressed in
a common life together and a common responsibility to God for His work in the world. It is true
that the number of the elect is known only to God
and that the bonds of the true Church are not
co-terminous with those of the visible Church, but

[1] *Divided Christendom*, pp. 48–63.

[2] As the second half of the same chapter, pp. 64–92,
where he discusses the oneness of the visible form of the
Church, reveals.

[3] Ibid., pp. 51–2.

it is also true that a Christian unity which is not expressed in this life in the only place where it can be fully expressed, in the society of the visible Church, is a sentimental delusion. To all who have some understanding of the Biblical doctrine of the Church this is, of course, obvious, but it seems necessary to say it because much modern Anglo-Saxon Protestantism does not appear prepared to accept it. There are many 'Free' Churchmen who regard a federation of Churches in which divisions in Christ's Body are accepted as normal, if not indeed desirable, as the goal to which movements towards Re-union should aim, and while it is true that many of Father Congar's shrewd criticisms of the 'branch' theory of the Church so popular among certain Anglo-Catholics[1] are valid only from the point of view of the peculiar Roman Catholic conception of the Church's oneness, nevertheless he does succeed in proving that the Church of England is not prepared to take the unity of the Church with full Biblical seriousness. Nor is it possible to take refuge behind the idea which practical ecclesiastics, impressed by the way in which each tradition is firmly entrenched in its own distinctive ways, so frequently put forward, that different Churches serve a useful purpose in the providence of God because each makes its unique contribution to the many-sided richness of the manifestation of Christ to the world which would be impossible if all Churches 'had all things

[1] *Divided Christendom*, pp. 181–97.

common'. As Barth puts it, 'The New Testament speaks of a variety of communities, of gifts and of persons within the one Church. But this manifoldness has no independent significance. . . . Like the unity of the Church it has its basis in God's grace, and in no second principle distinguishable from grace. It is indeed, in itself, nothing else than the living unity of grace, the one body of Christ in the actuality of its members and organs. In the New Testament, therefore, we find no relation of polarity or tension, or of mutual dependence, between the one Church and the many gifts, persons and the like; we find only a one-sided relation of dependence and derivation in which the many are subordinate to the one.'[1] In the present confused and disrupted state of the Church, therefore, where many bodies, all of which bear some of the marks of catholicity, cannot hold communion with each other and yet cannot deny the name of Churches to each other, we must confess that it lacks the very first of the qualities which reveal its distinctively catholic character. This is especially true of the different branches of the Church in England, which are living in a state of open sin. Not only are they divided from each other—in certain circumstances schism may seem to be the least of a number of evils—but they have acquiesced in their divisions and have fallen into the gravest

[1] *The Church and the Churches* (James Clarke & Co.), pp. 15–17.

of all contradictions of true catholicity, that of
'denominationalism'.[1]

The Catholic Church in its fullness, therefore,
must be one Church. At the same time its unity
must be based on the Word and Sacraments and
on 'the structure of catholicism' as they witness
to Jesus Christ. This needs to be emphasized as
against certain tendencies in the Oecumenical
Movement, which Congar has exposed so devasta-
tingly,[2] though, as he admits, they are now dis-
appearing. Barth has again made the significant
point. He reminds us that the quest for the one
Church cannot be concerned with the 'magical
fascination of numerical unity or uniqueness, nor
with the ethical and social ideals of uniformity,
mental harmony and agreement'. If it were a quest
for such 'Church-unity in itself' we should find
that, as he shrewdly remarks, both the powers of
sin and the powers of grace were against us irre-
sistibly. 'The quest for the unity of the Church
must, in fact, be identical with the quest for Jesus
Christ as the concrete Head and Lord of the

[1] 'Denominationalism' is the attitude of a Church which
ceases to scrutinize and reform itself under the Word of
God and loses all concern about its catholicity, contenting
itself with enjoying and perpetuating its own traditions and
distinctive ethos and maintaining itself in separation from
other Churches not for theological reasons but because 'it
prefers its own way of doing things'. The attitude is by
no means confined, therefore, to the 'Free' Churches in
England.

[2] *Divided Christendom*, ch. iv.

Church. Jesus Christ as the one Mediator between God and man *is* the oneness of the Church, is that unity within which there may be a multiplicity of communities, of gifts, of persons within one Church, while through it a multiplicity of Churches are excluded.'[1] Once again, it is the personal presence of Jesus Christ which is alone the source of the Church's catholicity.

Secondly, a Catholic Church will have the quality of what Professor Clement Rogers calls 'universality of appeal', though its appeal will certainly not be to the 'groundwork of certain instincts common to all men,'[2] but that which is alone truly fundamental in all men, their rediscovery of the essence of human nature in the intention of God through their incorporation into the Divine Humanity of Jesus Christ. The life of the Church should so make manifest Jesus Christ that any Christian from any place, no matter how different the accidents of the life of his own Church might be, should be able, once he had adapted himself to his new surroundings, to recognize his Lord as present in its midst and feel entirely at home in it as 'the household of faith'. It is despite the differences of temperament and interest and background and loyalty which normally divide men rather than because, as Professor Rogers imagines, of the instincts they have in common that all men should find themselves at home

[1] *Knowledge of God and Service of God*, pp. 17–19.
[2] *A Church Genuinely Catholic*, p. 156.

in the Church, because she draws her life not from the confused, distorted character of fallen human nature but from Jesus Christ Who 'brake down the middle wall of partition' that 'he might create in himself of the twain one new man, so making peace'.[1]

Here, once more, the example of the Roman Church is a reproach to modern Protestantism. There may be a good deal of special pleading in Newman's eloquent contrast of the universal appeal of the Roman Church with the limited and sectarian appeals of other Churches, but there is enough truth in it to give an edge to his observations.[2] The Reformed Churches in England, and this is true of the Church of England also, lacking 'the structure of catholicism' in the sense we have defined in any well-articulated form, have had little to help them resist the *Zeitgeist* or the attitude of their particular class or social tradition and consequently it has been only those who have been possessed with the *Zeitgeist*, or who belonged to their particular class or social tradition, who have felt any affinity with them. But we must insist again that 'the structure of catholicism' must be understood in the sense we have defined, as expressing the criticism of the Lord of the Church upon the Church so that the Church makes manifest His Lordship and that alone. The Roman

[1] Eph. ii. 14, 15.
[2] *Discourses to Mixed Congregations*, quoted in Przywara, *A Newman Synthesis*, pp. 93–5.

Church, because she is unable to distinguish between the action of Christ and the action of the hierarchy, is compelled to regard the maintenance of her own existence as an organization as her first concern, and is thus driven to tie herself in many countries to a social and political and cultural order which in no way make manifest the Lordship of Christ. Once more, it is the presence of Christ and that alone which ensures the Church's 'universality of appeal'.

This does not mean, of course, that particular congregations and even particular national Churches should not in some ways reflect the character of the environment in which they are set. On the contrary, it would be a sure sign of a Church's lack of effective impact upon the community in which it was set if it did not.[1] But it does mean that the Church should always strive to keep local characteristics in their proper place and not permit them to obscure her catholicity. She must always ensure that Jesus Christ has the primacy in her own midst and that her people are faithful to her because they are faithful to Jesus Christ and not because of her central place in the social life of the neighbourhood or her unique position as the repository of the national traditions. The attitude of many Welsh Nationalists to their chapels and that of many

[1] Congar, for instance, shows us how even in the Roman Church, 'in every country the Church has its own back ground and customs, its own clergy and institutions. *Divided Christendom*, pp. 106–7.

Italian Fascists to the Roman Church, fundamentally similar as they are, are not a source of strength to their respective Churches. They are signs that their Churches have not distinguished sharply enough between the Church's essence and the accidents of her life in a particular place, that they have, in fact, been guilty of precisely that concentration on non-essentials which is the sure mark of the absence of catholicity and, hence, of the presence of a false church.

Thirdly, a truly catholic Church will permit nothing in its constitution which hinders it in its obedience to the Word of God. The most obvious and common of these hindrances is State control. There can be no excuse in any circumstances for the Church's accepting dictation regarding its distinctively ecclesiastical actions from an entirely different and essentially mundane body such as the State. No matter how Christian the State may happen to be, no matter how strenuously it may endeavour to ensure that all who hold office in it are sincere members of the Church, the functions of Church and State, according to the ordinance of God, remain different functions, and it is essential to the proper working of both that the distinction between them be clearly understood. The State should recognize and protect the Church and the Church should acknowledge the responsibility and relative authority of the State, but the Church should never allow the State to become a Church nor the State allow the Church to become a State.

We recognize that the English Establishment is a very embarrassing legacy to modern members of the Church of England and that they are not to be held responsible for the sins of their fathers, although we are compelled to note that there are many in that Church who are still openly impenitent. We recognize, too, that an agitation for freedom from State control at the present juncture might be completely misunderstood and do more harm than good. 'Free' Churchmen must be sympathetic and not scornful to those Anglicans who are genuinely troubled by the present situation. But we are bound to confess ourselves at a loss to understand how a Church can proclaim boldly and sometimes even complacently that she possesses the marks of catholicity and, in particular, the Apostolic Succession, when even her ministers are appointed by a now secularized State, not infrequently with a flagrant disregard for the Church's wishes. Surely, if any action of the Church is distinctively her own and demands the leading of God's Holy Spirit—as traditional Catholicism itself has always rightly insisted—it is that of discerning whether her ministers are in truth called of God and ratifying their appointment. And it is merely frivolous to take cover behind the argument that bishops can refuse to consecrate a suitable nominee, or behind the very English fiction of the *congé d'élire*. A Church which is in earnest about her catholic status will make absolutely sure that she possesses both the formal and the real right to appoint her own ministers. And to justify the present procedure by claiming that, on the whole, 'it works out all right in practice' is simply to assert that 'the structure of catholicism' is a matter of indifference and that Church Order is not of Divine appointment.

At the same time, however, it should be said against those 'Free' Churchmen who make such a bogey of State interference that, in effect, they deny any theological significance to the State at all, that it is a sign of catholicity if the Church recognizes and honours the State when it is fulfilling its proper function as the State according to God's ordinance for it. It has not even been the serious perfectionism of what Troeltsch calls the 'sect-type' of Christianity which has prompted the indifference of most of the 'Free' Churches in modern times to the State. It has been merely a combination of traditional Liberal political theory with a provincial and impressionistic conception of the Gospel and the Church which failed to understand the theological necessity of the State[1] or the relevance of the Gospel to the whole structure of society.

It is important, also, to realize that other powers than that of the State can hinder the Church's obedience to her Lord unless she is vigilant against them. It is possible for a class interest or a financial interest or a dominating personality to impose its

[1] As expounded in Barth, *Church and State* (S.C.M., 1939).

will upon the Church, and this will be the more deadly when it is not open and flagrant but, as frequently happens, when it is sincere and quite unconscious. Archdeacon Grantley, with his warm attachment, as Rector of Plumstead Episcopi and son of the old Bishop of Barchester, to the anomalies in the distribution of the temporalities of the Church of England and his consuming desire to see his son established as a substantial country gentleman, was undoubtedly a sincere and devoted Churchman. In the same way, few Church leaders in Wales appear to be in any way conscious of how completely socially conditioned their various denominations are, with the 'Free' Churches expressing the spirit of the dominant indigenous Welsh democracy and the Church of England in Wales that of the Anglicized members of the middle-classes and the Roman Catholic Church that of the Irish immigrants. And once again, the only safeguard against this obscuring of the distinctive marks of the Church of God is standing under the discipline and crisis of the Word of God as it is in the Scriptures. It is Jesus Christ Himself Who can alone set His Church free for its own task of making manifest His Lordship.

Fourthly, a truly Catholic Church will permit nothing in the form of its intellectual life which hinders it from its obedience to its Lord. It will take seriously the fact that its Gospel, God's Word in Jesus Christ, is indeed catholic truth and that, therefore, it is universally valid, so that all other truths derive from it. It is in this sense and in this sense only that the Word can be thought of as Universal Reason, and certainly not in the sense of the immanent principle of the natural order of being which exists in some way in its own right independently of that Eternal Word which is the same Word as God speaks to man in Jesus Christ. Because the Word is thus the source of all truth the Church need have no fear that any truth, when seen in the light of the Word, need contradict the truth of the Gospel, nor need it take up a defensive attitude against truth in any form. Barth puts the point finely in dealing with the Church's attitude to the Bible. He is discussing the danger of exegesis becoming an imposition upon the Scriptures and not an exposition of them, and therefore degenerating into a mere conversation of the Church with herself, and he says that 'we shall not banish this danger, but only really begin to conjure it up and render it acute, by making right exposition depend upon the verdict of an ultimately decisive Church teaching office, or on the verdict of an historical and critical science, comporting itself with an equal infallibility. If we assume that the one or the other of these authorities is worthy of the Church's highest confidence, in both cases the Church makes a mistake about the Bible, so far that she thinks that in one way or another she can control right exposition and thereby set a norm over the norm, and ought to and can seize upon the norm for herself. Bible exegesis should be left open on all sides, not, as this demand was put by Liberalism, for the sake of free thinking, but for the sake of a free Bible.'[1] From one side, indeed, the function of critical Dogmatics in the Church may be described as that of removing intellectual hindrances from the Church's following of her Lord, and hence the freeing of the Church from the dangers of 'obscurantism', which is the denial of catholicity on the intellectual plane. The Churches which do not understand what critical Dogmatics means conspicuously fail to avoid this danger. The Roman Church, having committed itself in advance to the absolutizing of relative human language about God through the acceptance of an 'official' philosophy, is compelled—in practice, if not entirely in theory—to dogmatize about philosophical matters which are, very obviously, open questions. Even more strikingly, her erroneous conception of the nature of tradition and of inspiration drives her to assume not a wisely conservative but a merely timid and prosaic attitude in matters of Biblical Criticism which prevents her from reaping the benefits of the immeasurably more inward and vivid understanding of the Scriptures which Biblical Criticism, when seen in the right perspective, has helped us to achieve. Similarly, the notorious Doctrinal Report of the Church of England, whose ultimate principle of interpretation appears to be that elusive but all-pervasive entity 'the mind of the Church of England', shows an

[1] *Doctrine of the Word of God*, p. 119.

even greater theological obscurantism, with its unedifying compromises and its apparent inability to lay bare fundamental theological principles.[1] But 'Modernism' with its 'unfettered freedom of the enquiring human intelligence' avoids the danger still less. This means, as we have already seen, simply that the mind of 'modern' man is made the norm of catholic truth, and since, by definition, that mind is coloured at every point by its environment, the 'Modernist' is at the mercy of every change in mood of the age. And if he is not at pains to keep on the track of all the latest books or if, as has happened in the last ten years, the modern mood changes so sharply that it becomes unintelligible to those who allowed themselves to become completely conditioned by the mood of the previous generation, then 'Modernism' inevitably lapses into the irrelevance and obscurantism which is its bogey. There is no escape from this except to find the norm of truth outside the relativities of the age in which one lives. Many Christian 'Modernists' would agree with this and say that they find it in 'the Spirit of Jesus', but this means nothing unless they are prepared to accept the only safeguard which exists to prevent the 'Spirit of Jesus' being coloured beyond recognition by 'the spirit of the age', namely, the

[1] These defects are displayed throughout the Report, though less obviously in Part II than in Parts I and III. The sections on 'God and the World', I (A), and on the Resurrection, III (B)1, are striking examples.

witness of the Apostles and prophets as to its true nature.

Fifthly, and as the more positive side of our last point, the Catholic Church will try to declare 'the whole counsel of God'. She will try to grasp for herself the whole of the Faith and the relation of all its parts to each other and try to express it in such a way that it lights up the whole of human life. This is, of course, as indispensable a function of Dogmatics, as its other name, Systematic Theology, suggests, as the work of criticism and the Church is equally inarticulate and confused when it is not carried out. It is necessary, not merely for purposes of intellectual satisfaction in the limited sense, but also in order that men may know God's will for the world and that the relevance of the Gospel to all our life in all its parts may be clearly seen. From this point of view English theology— and this is peculiarly true of the Church of England, which frequently preens itself on its lack of interest in Systematic Theology[1] and has hardly any professional chairs at its universities on the subject—is seriously deficient in one of the most important qualities of catholicity. It was Moses,

[1] Christian ethics, both personal and social, come, of course, under the heading of Systematic Theology. It is significant that in the University of Oxford, until very recently indeed, lectures on Dogmatic Theology normally meant historical analyses of the teaching of the Fathers, while, although there were over fifty theological teachers in the university, no-one ever lectured on Christian Social Doctrine.

not Aaron, who was 'slow of speech and of a slow tongue', and Aaron, who 'spoke well', was appointed of the Lord to speak for him. The ordinary Church member may be permitted to continue to observe the English custom of being inarticulate on the subject of one's deepest beliefs, but it is sheer unadulterated laziness on the part of his ministers when they try to do the same.

Sixthly, and as the corollary of the Church's fullness of proclamation, a catholic Church will have fullness of liturgical life. This, of course, does not mean, as it is popularly taken to mean, that a Church will necessarily have a very formalized service, with read prayers and elaborate ceremonial. It means simply that the Church, in her λειτουργία, will make manifest all the many-sided richness of Christ in the same way as she declares 'the whole counsel' of God in her proclamation, which is itself an aspect of her λειτουργία. This whole approach to the question of Divine Service has been lost sight of in our English tradition because of the tiresome disputes about the Prayer Book and its attempt to establish uniformity of worship and the quite secondary question of the relative merits of 'set' and extempore prayer. We owe a great deal to the Liturgical Movement in Roman Catholicism and to such sympathetic exponents of it in England as Father Hebert for reminding us of the more positive significance of the Liturgy, in its wider meaning of the devotional life of the Church as a whole, as well as in the more fundamental sense of 'the institutions and ordinances of Christ in the outward worship of God' already discussed. John Owen, in his *Discourse Concerning Liturgies*,[1] lays down several important theological principles for our attitude towards Divine Service, but we cannot help feeling that his polemical interest makes him unnecessarily truculent in refusing to discuss what we may describe as the secondary content of Divine Service, a refusal which has caused English Protestantism to suffer incalculable impoverishment in its worship to this day. His argument against the claim that 'set forms' are indispensable to worship and that no addition must on any account be made to them is devastating. He is surely right in asserting that 'the adminstration of gospel ordinances consists in prayers, thanksgiving, instruction, and exhortations, suitably applied unto the special nature and end of the several ordinances themselves, and the use of them in the Church',[2] and in claiming that for the right performance of all these Christ gives gifts unto his ministers, whereas the *binding* of ministers to 'set forms', which are 'man-made' and require only the gifts of being able to read and speak properly, effectively prevents the ministers from exercising the spiritual gifts with which Christ has endowed them. At the same time, he does not ask himself whether the nature of the 'Gospel ordinances' themselves does not compel

[1] Works, *Discourse Concerning Liturgies*, vol. xix.
[2] Ibid., p. 454.

the Church's service to take a certain form so that that form, although not actually found in Scripture, is yet not merely 'man-made' but an inevitable development, an exegesis, of the 'Gospel ordinances'. The structure of the Reformed Service, with the Sacrament of the Lord's Supper, is the obvious example. It need not necessarily be stereotyped in a printed order—there are weighty reasons why a certain freedom should be allowed the minister, though there is no reason why we should rule out the possibility of the Spirit guiding men in producing a printed order, especially when it is based on traditional forms—but it is difficult to deny that the logic of the Gospel itself seems to demand that the Reformed Service contain confession, absolution, the reading of the Word, intercessions, the preaching of the Word, the reading of the Words of Institution, the Anaphora, the Prayer of Consecration, the Epiklesis, the Communion, in more or less that order and that the service is not a 'full' service when any of these are missing. Similarly, the commemoration of the significant 'moments' of our redemption in the Christian Year, while not itself one of the 'Gospel Ordinances', is obviously solidly based on the apostolic testimony, and therefore fulfils Owen's requirement that all parts of the Church's worship should be 'conducive to edification'. Once more, whether it is desirable to have a set lectionary or not, a 'gifted' minister will recognize a certain obligation to ensure that the salient portions of the Bible be read as a coherent unity[1] in the course of a year, in order that the Church may be helped to keep 'the proportion of faith'. And we can frankly admit that there is no doubt that Protestantism has lost much of what we may call without sentimentality or preciousness the poetry of the Church's life through its ignorance of the kind of significance that Father Hebert gives to ritual in Divine Service.[2]

Yet, once more, we have to insist that this fullness of liturgical life needs to be controlled at every point by the Gospel as it is in Scripture. As soon as the vital relation between Dogmatics and Liturgy is lost then the forms become meaningless and Divine Service a 'whited sepulchre'. The Liturgy does not stand alone and cannot be taken, as traditional Catholicism so frequently does take it, as an excuse for lack of interest in theology or for refusing to stir up the spiritual gifts with which Christ has endowed both minister and people. There is a significant passage in Hebert where he describes how, at the Counter-Reformation, 'the priest celebrating his silent Mass still repeated the remains of the ancient congregational chants, the Introit, Gradual and the rest, and recited offertory prayers implying the offering of the gifts by the

[1] Cf. the excellent observations on the liturgical use of the Psalms and Scriptures in Hebert, *Liturgy and Society*, pp. 214–22, though he does not say all that we should like to say about Preaching.

[2] Ibid., pp. 65–81.

people, and post-communion collects implying the communion of the people'.[1] Surely this is as great an abuse as that of modern neo-Protestantism, which makes no attempt to draw out the structure of Divine Service from the nature of the 'Gospel ordinances' themselves, but is concerned simply with 'getting across' to people and making its services 'interesting'?

Seventhly, as a further expression of her liturgical life a truly catholic Church will recognize her responsibility for forming a Christian pattern of society. We have to present our *bodies* as a λογική λατρεία, and the whole of our life, in all its parts —including its social and economic and political parts—must be fashioned, not according to the form of this world but according to its transformation, which we already know in faith in the life of the Church. This is, of course, linked on directly to our discussion earlier of the marks of the Catholic Christian. It would be beyond the scope of this study to discuss the exact sense in which we can speak of 'Christian civilization' or 'Christian culture', but it is obvious that we must be able to use these terms in some sense if we take seriously Christ's Lordship over the whole of life.[2] Similarly, as Brother George Every has recently pleaded,[3] there must be a relation between the

[1] Hebert, *Liturgy and Society,* pp. 117–18.
[2] It is frequently quite erroneously and arbitrarily supposed that Reformed theology can have no interest in these matters.   [3] *Christian Discrimination* (Sheldon Press, 1940.)

Gospel and good taste if Christ is truly God and truly Man. The fact that Christians in general have offered so little resistance to the steady vulgarization of the common life which modern mass society has achieved is one of the clearest indications of our lack of real belief in Christ as the Power through Whom and unto Whom all things have been created and in Whom they hold together.[1]

Finally, the most distinctive of all the qualities of a truly catholic Church will be her humility. The criterion which our Lord left us for distinguishing His true followers from the false was: 'By their fruits ye shall know them.' And, as we have seen, the Church must not only possess 'the structure of catholicism', she must prove in her own life that she understands that structure and is allowing it to fulfil its proper function. Because of this, a truly catholic Church will not be too ready boldly to assert its own catholicity. The poverty of its fruits will remind it that, at best, it provides but 'stony ground' for the seed of the Word. And the last thing it will be able to do will be to 'glory' in its history or its liturgical forms or its 'orthodox' teaching or its recognition by other Churches, since all these things, when truly understood, remind it only of how far it falls short of its high calling in Jesus Christ.[2] It is significant

[1] Col. i. 16–17.
[2] Cf. The excellent observation in Ramsey, *The Gospel and the Catholic Church*, pp. 44–5, on the connection between humility and membership of the Body.

that in the second chapter of Philippians the idea of membership of the Body is inseparably linked up with having the 'same mind' as was also in Christ Jesus, Who 'being found in fashion as a man, humbled himself'. 'A disciple is not above his master nor a servant above his lord. It is enough for the disciple that he be as his master, and the servant as his lord.'[1] 'The form of a servant', humility, is, therefore, the most appropriate quality of a Church which lays claim to be catholic.

[1] Matt. x. 24–25a.

Chapter VI

CATHOLICITY IN ENGLAND TO-DAY

As was emphasized in our first chapter, the Church situation in England to-day is in the melting-pot, and any attempt to range Churches against each other breaks down. According to the analysis of the nature of catholicity we have tried to give, no Church in England can claim to be a 'Church genuinely Catholic' and, therefore, no Church can conceive of the situation simply in terms of converting other Churches to its own point of view. So confused, indeed, has the situation become that the traditional Reformed Churches, the Presbyterian and the Congregational, which should, in theory, be the most catholic, have been in practice so riddled with secular 'denominationalism' that they have become far less genuinely catholic than many parts of the Church of England, whose constitution almost prevents it from making the attempt to achieve catholicity. There are few matters in which the 'Gilbertian' English temperament is more the despair of the logically consistent than in matters ecclesiastical.

One fact is clear, however. No branch of the Church in England, with the exception of the Roman Church, maintains any longer that it is the exclusive possessor of catholicity. All the major Churches acknowledge that the others are in some sense real Churches. The writings of such representative and highly respected Anglo-Catholics as Bishop Gore and Dr. T. A. Lacey make this perfectly clear from the side of the most serious adherents of traditional Catholicism, while the famous Lambeth Appeal to all Christian people of 1920 has expressed authoritatively the mind of the Church of England as a whole. And the acceptance of the 'Affirmation of union in allegiance to our Lord Jesus Christ' made by the Faith and Order Conference at Edinburgh in 1937 by the representatives of all the English Churches except the Roman does at least mean, if words mean anything, that they do accept each other as fellow Christians and, therefore, their respective Churches as, in some sense, real Churches. For the most part, the main concern of the 'Free' Churches in recent years has been not so much to challenge the right of other bodies to the name of Church as to defend their own right to that name.

This, of course, is widely acknowledged, but there have been few signs as yet that its immense significance for the future of the traditional Catholic doctrine of the Church has been pondered very deeply. The Roman Church, which still insists on communion with the See of Rome as the distinctive mark of catholicity, has no need to reconsider her position, but Anglo-Catholics, in particular, are surely compelled to examine again the whole foundation of the doctrine of the Church as they have been accustomed to expound it. If the episcopal ministry is not imperatively necessary to the Church's life, since churches can at least exist and bear some of the marks of catholicity without it, then in what does the essence of the Church consist?[1] We suspect that the Church of England has not yet really made up its mind on this matter. Much of its attachment to the monarchical episcopate appears to an outsider to be due partly to an innate conservatism and partly to a desire to cling to it as the one tangible mark of traditional Catholicism which at the same time links it with

---

[1] This is not the too-familiar discussion whether episcopacy is of the *esse* or the *bene esse* of the Church. Perhaps it clarifies the discussion to put the question in terms of our own argument. Is the Ministry itself part of the Gospel so that the voice of the bishop is always without ambiguity the voice of Christ, and since Christ is the essence of the Church, is the Ministry also of the essence of the Church? This, of course, is the Roman position and the one which the Church of England has apparently rejected. Or is the Ministry an effective means of ensuring the faithful proclamation of the Gospel, which yet exists independently of it, so that a Church without it would lack the Church's fullness without necessarily ceasing altogether to be a Church? Such a Church would possess the raw material of catholicity but in an undifferentiated and inarticulate form and hence be very exposed to the danger of corruption.

the other traditionally Catholic Churches and distinguishes it from the English 'Free' Churches rather than to a clearly-apprehended theological conviction. But if the Church of England is prepared to reject the Roman identification of the magisterium of the hierarchy with that of Jesus Christ Himself and to acknowledge that the authority of the Ministry in the Church is held under the κρίσις of the Word of God as declared by the Apostles in the Scriptures, as it seems she is, then where does she discern the primary marks of catholicity? It is difficult to see how she can give a different answer from our own, namely, in the presence of the Word and Sacraments as they make manifest the presence of Jesus Christ. And it is difficult to see, further, what the Church of England would stand to lose by making such an answer. If the Church of England is prepared to make explicit in her theological teaching what is already implicit in her ecclesiastical practice, then, speaking from within Independency, we see no theological objection to our reaching agreement on the doctrine of the Ministry, however serious practical difficulties in the way of immediate re-union may be. We freely admit that the Church of England can contribute at least as much—and in some ways a great deal more—as the 'Free' Churches to our understanding of the doctrine of the Ministry, and indeed that we shall not be able to reach a doctrine of the Ministry in England which is both truly reformed and catholic without the contribution of the Church of England. We can teach each other much, and we need each other's lessons, while we must all learn again together the meaning of reformation according to the Word of God and the true relation between the Gospel and Church Order.

There are two serious difficulties in the way of our achieving catholicity in the Church in England, difficulties which are, however, offset by two hopeful signs. The first is the degeneration, both formally and materially, of the 'Free' Churches. It is true that there has been no obvious formal deterioration in the Presbyterian Churches, which, in both England and Scotland, have retained a coherent and self-consistent Church Order which possesses a catholic sweep and claims to base itself solidly on the Scriptures; but even the Presbyterian Churches have frequently succumbed to the corrosive influence of Liberalism, and the significance of Reformed Church Order has been as frequently misunderstood in their midst as in Churches less fortunately placed in regard to their outward form. The characteristic sin of the modern 'Free' Churches has been 'denominationalism'. This we defined earlier as the attitude of a Church more interested in enjoying and perpetuating its own distinctive traditions and atmosphere than in bringing itself under the Word of God as it is declared in Scripture, and thus making manifest Christ's Lordship, and it has, perhaps, been more prevalent in modern England than anywhere else, with the possible exception of America. It is almost a commonplace to say that the Churches in England are no longer divided on theological grounds —which are, when understood in their proper existential significance, the only valid grounds for schism in Christ's Church—but because they each represent a particular type of 'devotional life' or 'form of worship' or even 'social stratum'. Having lost the principle of reformation according to the Word of God the English 'Free' Churches have striven to reform themselves according to 'modern thought' or 'the spirit of the age', and it is these rather than 'the structure of catholicism' which have controlled the development of their modern forms of Church organization. This is strikingly illustrated by the characteristic organization of modern Congregationalism, the Congregational Union of England and Wales. This body carefully avoids, in fact if not altogether in theory, making confessional agreement the basis on which its constituent Churches unite. The result is that it becomes a complete expression of the spirit of 'denominationalism'. A man might be a fully-equipped Reformed theologian, with wide experience of proper ecclesiastical administration, but unless he understood the peculiar ethos of 'Congregationalism' he would be almost entirely lost in an assembly of the Congregational Union because its procedure is not controlled by any recognizable theological canons. Conversations about re-union become impossible with a body of this kind because it has no apparent responsibility to anything but the whims of its own members. It is true that the Union is formally responsible to individual Churches which are committed to obedience to the Lord Jesus Christ, and that among its 'objects' are 'to extend and realize the Kingdom of Christ, primarily through Churches of the Congregational Order' and 'To promote New Testament principles of Church fellowship and organization',[1] but, as the very wording of these quotations suggests, it is an organization which exists to serve the purposes of the Church rather than the Church itself, existing in one of its own forms, and therefore avoids the direct responsibility to her Lord which 'the structure of catholicism' is designed to preserve for the Church in all her actions. One of the first conditions of re-union and of the establishment of a 'Church genuinely Catholic' in this country is the rediscovery by the Reformed Churches of their own true foundation and the bringing of their whole Church Order into conformity with God's ordinance for His Church.

The second difficulty is the curious position of the Church of England. Now the Church of England is, in many ways, the most anomalous institution in the world, and perhaps the safest generalization we can make about it is that it is not safe to make any generalizations. It has to be remembered, also,

[1] 'Constitution of the Congregational Union of England and Wales', Section III. Printed in the Congregational Year Book.

that the present members of the Church of England were not responsible for formulating their Church's constitution and that few tasks can be more complex, both in their political and ecclesiastical ramifications, than that of reforming the structure of the Church of England and its relation to the State at the present time. Nevertheless, the very complexity of that task is itself a striking indication of the nature of our difficulty. For the entity called the Church of England, from one point of view, can hardly be called a Church at all. Strictly speaking, it is a *settlement* of the 'religious question' in England, proposed and, partly, enforced by the State, which a large number of churchmen accepted. 'When Elizabeth came to the throne in 1558,' Dr. Bicknell tells us,[1] 'she had a hard task before her. Her aim must be to secure religious unity at home in the face of many active and powerful enemies abroad. She began not with questions of doctrine, but of worship and discipline. She recovered from Parliament the restoration of the Royal Supremacy: enforced by Act of Parliament the restoration of the Prayer Book: filled up vacant sees: took strong measures to enforce a modicum of decency in worship.' And her successors, whether from the throne or in Parliament, have proceeded in very much the same manner down to 1928 and to this present day. The Church of England is, apparently, not there-

[1] E. J. Bicknell, *Theological Introduction to the Thirty-Nine Articles* (Longmans'), p. 17.

fore a Church, concerned in all things to acknowledge the Supreme Headship of Jesus Christ, but
an instrument for securing 'religious unity at home
in the face of many active and powerful enemies
abroad'. It is a working compromise which keeps
the peace in theological matters and discourages
the possibility of debate on certain questions because they threaten to disturb the peace.

Now, of course, we are fully aware, as we have
freely and gladly admitted throughout this study,
that the Church of England bears many marks of
the Church Catholic and that there is probably far
more genuine concern for catholicity in the Church
of England at present than in almost any other
Church, but we are bound to press the seriousness
of this point because so many members of the
Church of England appear to be completely obli-
vious of it. Theoretically, we suppose it might be
possible for the Church of England to reject the
religious settlement, as did the Ejected Ministers
in 1662, if she wished to—though that is very
doubtful—and thus she may be able to claim that
she has not really surrendered her right to rule,
under Christ, in her own house, but we are bound
to inquire, as we did earlier, whether the very
character of that settlement is such that, in effect,
it does not mean the giving up of that right. If the
King in Parliament is in a position to control
appointments to the responsible Ministry of the
Church, then he can obviously ensure that the
settlement is maintained and the critical activity

of reformation according to the Word of God discouraged. No Church which is concerned to preserve 'the structure of catholicism' in the sense we have given it can accept such a situation.

Because of this, the Church of England has, in some ways, become a 'denomination' *par excellence*. In one sense, at least, it can be said that no Church in Christendom is less catholic than the Church of England. Few Anglo-Catholics would deny that in the Church of England the 'structure of catholicism' has been subtly distorted, unconsciously maybe, but none the less effectively, in order, not to make manifest Christ's Lordship, but to maintain the 'religious settlement' and to cohere easily with the rest of the national life. Thus the English episcopate has frequently been primarily concerned, not with the proper ministerial function of defining the apostolic testimony and keeping Church proclamation pure by constant scrutiny under the light of the Word of God, but with avoiding at all costs making a definite pronouncement regarding the nature of that testimony lest the unity of the Church of England be broken. On occasion, Anglican bishops have openly regarded themselves as civil servants whose purpose it is to adminster the 'religious settlement'. This, of course, has its inevitable ramifications in the theological sphere. Certain modern Anglican theologians, and they are not always confined to the ranks of the 'Modern Churchmen', tend to speak as though the criterion of theological truth is not

'What saith the Scriptures?' or even 'What saith the Catholic Church?' but 'the mind of the Church of England'. This is denominationalism pure and simple.[1]

The reformation of the Church of England, therefore, is as imperative a condition of re-union as the internal reformation of the 'Free' Churches. The Church of England must decide what it is and take steps to ensure that it possesses the right to be itself. We sympathize with the Anglo-Catholic who, when confronted by the confusion of modern Congregational Churches, protests that he cannot discuss re-union with such a group because no-one seems to know exactly what he is being asked to re-unite with, but we must insist that we also are in a similar position in regard to the Church of England. Indeed, we must assert that the confusion of the Church of England is worse, because there is ultimately a Congregational doctrine of the Church to be stated and an organ of responsible Church government to be found in

[1] It is interesting to observe that this is precisely the same attitude, in a different setting, as that of those Congregationalists who, when consulted on a point of doctrine or order, speak not of what Scripture and Tradition, which reaches self-consciousness in Dogmatic Theology, say but of what 'the practice among modern Congregational Churches is'. The 'religious settlement' in England has, apparently, done its work so well that it has succeeded even in making the 'dissident Dissenters' surrender their distinctive principle of Reformation according to the Word of God and copy its method and outlook!

a Congregational Church, but apparently an un-
ambiguous and universally acceptable definition
of the nature of the Church of England has never
been given, and it seems that reformation of the
Church of England cannot be carried out by anyone except the King in Parliament.[1] 'The Church
of England' of which many Anglo-Catholics speak
is often the Church they would like to see in
England rather than the one which in fact exists.
Before re-union can become a practical possibility,
therefore, the Church of England must reach an
understanding with the State which ensures its
spiritual freedom. We are prepared to discuss
re-union with a Church which can speak for itself,
but it would be an open denial of our own catholicity to treat with Caesar, even so high-handed a
Caesar as the British Parliament, concerning the
things which belong unto God and unto God
alone.[2]

[1] 'The Church cannot disestablish itself; it can only ask
for Disestablishment; and much would depend upon the
terms and conditions upon which Disestablishment was
granted.' *Church and State*, Report of the Archbishops'
Commission, 1935, p. 50.

[2] This will mean the rejection of the basis of the Anglican Establishment on the part of the Church of England
(*vide* the evidence of Professor J. M. Creed before the
Archbishops' Commission, *Church and State*, vol. ii, p.
239), but apparently the Bishops of the Church of England
are prepared to do this, since they state that 'it is a fundamental principle that the Church . . . must in the last
resort . . . retain its inalienable right, in loyalty to our
Lord and Saviour Jesus Christ, to formulate its faith in

This difficulty is closely related to the first of our hopeful signs, and indeed makes it as much a source of danger as of hope. The hopeful sign is that there is in this country a growing understanding of the need for finding true community and for re-creating a Christian pattern of life in society. This is linked up with a rediscovery of catholicity because, as we have seen, the Church is the true humanity and must strive to bring all parts of life under the dominion of God her Lord. As it has been said, 'The re-union of our disintegrated civilisation, which would mean the union, for the first time, of all human civilisation, awaits the re-union of the Christian Church and the evangelisation of the world.'[1] And in our own country at least we are beginning to see both that an obligation rests upon us to express our membership of the Church in terms of the common life and that, when we see our Christian vocation in that light, our ecclesiastical divisions have little reality. Our problems and responsibilities are common problems and responsibilities, it is the same people with whom we have to deal and we are confronted by the same temptations and opportunities. With our gradual re-discovery of our true nature as the Church, the political and social and

Him and to arrange the expression of that Holy Faith in its form of worship.' (Statement of Archbishop Davidson in the Church Assembly, 2 July 1928, quoted in *Church and State*, vol. i, p. 1).

[1] Hebert, *Unity and the Truth*, p. 63.

moral obstacles to re-union are falling into their properly subordinate places and the essential unity of those who bear the marks of the Lord Jesus Christ in our midst as against those who do not is being increasingly made clear. This is, in itself, a hopeful sign and should be welcomed as such by all who are concerned for the Church's catholicity.

But the danger is that the impetus which the movement towards re-union receives from this source may serve to strengthen the tendency which we have already noted for 'practical' churchmen to work for a re-union of vaguely ecclesiastical bodies in which 'the structure of catholicism' will be lost. Unless we are very careful—and the war will do much to intensify the danger—we shall have a new 'National' Church with a constitution fashioned with an eye on Parliamentary assent which will express 'the distinctive temper of the English people' much more clearly than the Church of England is able to in these days, and which will be a much more insidious form of 'denominationalism' than anything which we possess at present. That this is no fantasy is proved by the appearance in 1938 of the semi-official 'Outline Scheme for a Re-united Church', which Father Hebert has so convincingly exposed in his pamphlet *Unity and the Truth*. The well-meaning theological confusion of the attitude which produced that scheme, together with the ambiguous traditional Anglican conception of the 'Christian

Nation',[1] swept along by a wave of sentiment evoked by an experience of national unity in war-time may very well create a re-united Church of England which those who have a genuine concern for catholicity will be able only to deplore. Because of this, we must be grateful for the intransigent, if occasionally somewhat arrogant, attitude which the Church of England, paradoxically enough, has frequently taken up in regard to such matters as Intercommunion and mutual recognition of minis-tries. It has, at least, been a salutary reminder to us that the Order of Christ's Church is of Divine appointment and is not to be adjusted to our human convenience.

The surest way of guarding against this danger, however, is by rediscovering the inwardness of the 'structure of catholicism', and that can only be rediscovered by asking ourselves what the essence of the Church's catholicity is, and that, as we have tried to show, can be found only by standing under the Word of God in Jesus Christ, as He is declared to us through the testimony of the Apostles. The renewal of the study of theology, therefore, as 'the Church's concentrated anxiety and concern about her most intimate responsibility' is our most urgent task at the present time, and perhaps the growing revival of theological study is the most hopeful sign of a return of catholicity to our life as the

[1] Cf. a very interesting memorandum by Mr. Robert Stokes on this subject in *Church and State*, vol. ii, pp. 255–71.

Church in England to-day. As we said in our first chapter, the greatest hindrance to our making any progress in the direction of re-union in England has been our obstinate refusal to discuss the doctrine of the Church theologically and our readiness to fasten on secondary or irrelevant considerations as an excuse for perpetuating divisions. It is this which has made so much inter-denominational discussion fruitless and apparently unprofitable. But let us begin to ask ourselves seriously what the apostolic testimony is and the relation of the Church to it, and we shall have established genuine contact with each other. As soon as we stand together under the Word of God in the Scriptures then we are inevitably united in the 'Catholicism of the Word' and committed together to Reformation according to the Word of God. It is because this is beginning to happen that we can approach the future with confidence. As Father Hebert puts it, 'It is here, in fact, that the real strength of the Re-union movement lies, in the deepened grasp of the meaning of Christian dogma to which our generation is being driven in the conflict with anti-Christian forces. The movement back to a stronger hold on theology is taking place in the different denominations on parallel lines—or rather on converging lines, since the Gospel of God is one, and we are even now growing towards unity in the Truth.'[1]

That is indeed true, and because it is so it is

[1] *Unity and the Truth*, p. 60.

impossible to exaggerate the significance of the appearance of Sir Edwyn Hoskyns' *The Fourth Gospel*, incomplete as it is, for the future of catholicity in England. This book, written by a professed Anglo-Catholic under the influence of modern Reformed theology on the most 'theological' of the Gospels, provides us with the raw material for serious confessional discussion between Reformed and traditional Catholic theologians in England, because both can appeal to it with equal freedom. The solidly Biblical interest of Anglican theology has always been its saving grace, and our common willingness to stand under the discipline of Biblical theology as practised by Hoskyns is the most hopeful and enduring of our points of contact.

But, as a condition of continued effective discussion, one point must be clearly established. Anglican theology will have to make an effort to understand the distinctive method of Reformed theology. At present there are few signs that she does and many alarming signs that she does not. We are not sure how representative two articles on the 'Nature of Theology' by Father E. L. Mascall which appeared in *Theology* in the February and March numbers for 1941 are, but if they do show the direction which the new Anglican interest in Dogmatic Theology is taking, then there can be little hope of serious discussion between Anglican and Reformed theologians for a long time to come. We mentioned earlier that while Anglican theology strove always to base itself on the Scriptures, it yet showed little disposition to submit itself to the tremendous critical discipline which Reformed theology imposes upon itself in the effort to ensure that its exegesis of Scripture is precise and relevant. Father Mascall appears not so much to reject that discipline as to be completely ignorant of its existence. Dogmatic Theology to him is in no sense *critical* Theology. It is no more than the attempt merely to articulate the mind of the Church, formed admittedly by Scripture and Spirit-guided Tradition, at a particular time. This is certainly a step forward from Anglican Liberalism, both Catholic and Protestant, but ultimately it is precisely the same position as that of Father Congar and the Roman Church, and is intelligible only if the same identification of the Word of God with the Word of the Church is made. We have no right to complain of that position in itself— Father Mascall and the Roman Church may be correct in making such an identification—but, as far as we are concerned, profitable discussion with those who hold that position inevitably becomes impossible when they show themselves unaware of the nature of the Reformed criticism of it. It is difficult to take Father Mascall seriously when he airily identifies the teaching of Barth with the 'theologism' of the later Middle Ages and at the same time shows no appreciation of the significance for his own argument of the principle of Reformation according to the Word of God. We are inclined to labour this point because it is the biggest obstacle to our reaching an understanding even with those Anglican theologians with whom we have most in common. Discussion between Anglican and Reformed theologians cannot take place in an atmosphere of real confidence until Anglican theologians show signs of having mastered the argument of the Prolegomena to Barth's *Dogmatic*. And unless such discussion takes place, any reunion that will be achieved will be a denial and not a fulfilment of the Church's catholicity. The situation, as we have said, is perhaps more hopeful than it has ever been. But it is so only because we seem to be on the threshold of a new and richer understanding of what both Catholicism and Reformation mean. Our whole argument has been that if we concentrate our attention on one to the exclusion of the other we shall succeed in understanding neither. It may be, by the mercy of God, that we in England shall be able to make some reparation for the way in which we have all broken the unity of Christ's body in the past by taking advantage of the uncertain and anomalous position in which we find ourselves to-day to restore, more readily than is possible in other lands, the true 'structure of catholicism' in a reunited Church of Christ in England where all things minister to the glory of our Lord. But to do that, and to avoid making confusion worse confounded by not doing that, we must all make a genuine effort to understand exactly what each of us is trying to say.

Ubi Christus, ibi ecclesia. It is the testimony of the Apostles to what they have seen and heard and handled which gives the Church its commission and points it to the Source of its life and unity. Let us together give heed without ceasing to that testimony, not resting until He Who is its Subject declares His hidden Name to us, and it will surely happen that, finding ourselves anew in Him, we shall find each other, seeing each other only as we are found in Him. And when that takes place then all the foolish and blasphemous 'middle walls of partition' which separate us from each other will be broken down and, 'being built upon the foundation of the apostles and prophets, Christ Jesus himself being the chief corner stone', we shall become a true 'household of God', growing into 'a holy temple in the Lord', even 'a habitation of God in the Spirit'.

INDEX